Praise for *Gold Digge*

"Fascinating, terrifying, incredibly helpful — *Gold Diggers* is all that and more. I'll give this book to my daughter when she starts dating and I'd encourage every parent to do the same. And if you are in a relationship where something just doesn't seem right, read this book. It can save you a ton of money and heartache down the road."

~ GERRI DETWEILER, CREDIT EXPERT, AUTHOR,
AND HOST OF "TALK CREDIT RADIO"

"Candor, clear-cut advice, and a touch of healthy sarcasm make this book not only valuable but also fun to read. A serious topic and widespread problem are handled with delicately balanced humor and hardnosed reality. If you think you have been — or are about to be — the victim of financial abuse, it's well worth the read."

~ LOIS P. FRANKEL, PH.D., AUTHOR OF *NICE GIRLS DON'T GET RICH*

"*Gold Diggers and Dead Beat Dads* is the go-to financial guide when romantic love or family ties threaten to cloud your judgment. Savvy, insightful and sympathetic, Valerie Rind tackles taboo money matters without blame or scolding. Compelling accounts of lives upended by financial missteps and step-by-step action plans empower everyone to take charge of their financial future."

~ LEAH KLUNGNESS, PH.D., PSYCHOLOGIST AND
CO-AUTHOR OF *THE COMPLETE SINGLE MOTHER*

"Valerie Rind compassionately weaves compelling stories of well-meaning and often intelligent everyday people who fall prey to desperate and sociopathic friends, lovers and relatives. The true stories she shares, including her own, drive home the painful reality that not only can financial abuse befall anyone of us at any stage of life, but that there are also preemptive solutions and resources for survival. I'm recommending *Gold Diggers* to my young adult daughters as a cautionary tale of the real-life dangers that can follow when financial and emotional dependency converge."

~ BARRY PAPERNO, CREDIT EXPERT AND
WRITER AT *SPEAKINGOFCREDIT.COM*

"Every day I hear the stories of clients who have been financially betrayed by someone close to them. Their experiences are painful, humiliating, embarrassing and shame inducing. The first step in healing is to understand how easily it can happen to anyone and how deep the losses feel. In this book, Valerie Rind has bravely shared her own story and analyzed the stories of others to make sense of what happens when you are the victim of financial fraud from someone close to you. If you or someone you love has gone through this, read the book and share it. It happens more than you know."

~ Dr. Mary Gresham, financial psychologist

"Valerie Rind lost a lot of money at the hands of a deceitful ex. But she pulled her life back together and came out on top. In this book, Rind shares her experiences, but also skillfully weaves in stories of other men and women who lost money at the hands of someone they trusted. But this isn't just a tell-all. Writing in a witty and engaging style, Rind equips the reader with the knowledge they need to avoid these scenarios."

~ Beverly Harzog, consumer credit expert and
author of *Confessions of a Credit Junkie*

"*Gold Diggers and Deadbeat Dads* is a game changer in the world of personal finance education. By painting a picture of the many faces of financial abuse, Valerie Rind makes personal finance about personal responsibility again - rather than our insatiable need to people please and make others comfortable. Whether you are the co-signing sibling, ex-spouse of a deadbeat or enabling parent to a financially irresponsible adult, you'll read stories that prove you're not alone and, most importantly, that there is hope after having your assets kicked royally by the ones you love and the ones who claim to love you."

~ Patrice Washington, best-selling author of
Real Money Answers for Every Woman

Gold Diggers and Deadbeat Dads

True Stories of Friends, Family, *and* Financial Ruin

VALERIE RIND

Printed in the United States of America

First Printing, 2014

ISBN: 978-0-9906922-0-1 (paperback)
      978-0-9906922-1-8 (mobi)
      978-0-9906922-2-5 (ePub)

VSJ Enterprises, LLC
409 12th Street, SE
Washington, DC 20003

All names and other identifying details such as physical properties, occupations, and locations have been changed to protect the privacy of individuals.

Although the author and publisher have made every effort to ensure that the information in this book was correct at press time, the author and publisher do not assume and hereby disclaim any liability to any party for any loss, damage, or disruption caused by errors or omissions, whether such errors or omissions result from negligence, accident, or any other cause.

Links or references to external or third-party web sites are provided to readers solely as a convenience and for informational purposes only; they do not constitute an endorsement or an approval by the author or publisher. The author and publisher bear no responsibility for the accuracy, legality, or content of the external site or for that of subsequent links. Contact the external site for answers to questions regarding its content.

This book is not intended as a substitute for financial, investment, tax, accounting, psychological, or legal advice. The reader should consult the appropriately qualified professional advisors.

Cover design by Laura Duffy

Shovel image © iStock.com/wakila

Editing by Kathryn Holmes

Interior design by 1106 Design

Author photograph by Carl Bower

Dedication

To my ex-husband: Without you, I never would have written this book.

Table of Contents

Table of Contents

Introduction

What's a nice girl like me doing writing a book like this?

How could such a smart woman be so stupid? Sometimes I still can't believe it happened.

My husband spun a complex web of financial lies, ran up my credit card bills, and swindled me out of my life savings.

It wasn't entirely his fault. I loved and trusted him, but I didn't pay attention to the bright red flags that were flapping in the wind during our ten-year relationship.

I was thinking like a wife instead of thinking like a lawyer.

Why do I write about this topic?

My interest in people's stories of financial ruin caused by their friends or family members is not academic or professional.

It's personal. Extremely personal. I was wiped out after lending money to my husband for his startup business. Plus, I discovered that he'd kept a significant secret for nearly a decade.

When the truth hit the fan, I felt stupid. Angry. Embarrassed and ashamed.

Yet somehow I knew that a lot of people out there had been betrayed and had experienced the same roller coaster of emotions.

As a culture, we've brought physical abuse, verbal abuse, child abuse, sexual abuse, and domestic abuse out of the darkness. I hope to do the same for people who have suffered severe financial exploitation or misfortunes caused, at least in part, by their companions or relatives.

My goal is to show you that you're not alone.

I'll tell you all my "dirty little secrets." It's like watching a train wreck or reading the tabloids. You can't help but gawk at someone else's misfortune.

Go ahead, be a rubbernecker!

I am also honored and humbled that dozens of people revealed their private stories to me and allowed me to share them with you.

This book includes preventive tips to help you avoid common financial traps. You'll also learn how to deal with the aftermath of your monetary mistakes.

However, you should always consult the appropriate professionals for more specific advice about financial, investment, legal, tax, accounting, psychological, and other important life issues.

What is financial abuse or exploitation?

Economic setbacks can affect men and women, young and old, gay and straight, educated and illiterate, rich and poor. Virtually no one is immune. You wind up in debt, broke, or both.

All you need is a situation with three elements:

- A relationship built on trust

- Exploitation

- Loss of money or valuable assets, increased debt, or damage to credit.

Simply put — financial abuse occurs when friends or family members help you ruin your finances.

Financial abuse happens to lots of people, but no one ever talks about it. Victims often blame themselves. People tend not to report their downfalls — no one else gets scammed like this, right?

Wrong.

We're not alone in this clandestine club of folks who trusted others and got our assets kicked.

Here are some typical examples:

- After co-signing a car loan for his underemployed girlfriend, a recent college grad gets stuck with her debt. She drives off into the sunset, while his credit is ruined.

- A husband concealed the sorry state of the family's finances. Now, his young widow is a penniless single mother who can't even balance a checkbook.

- A man talks his wife into investing in a new technology venture. Instead, he loses all their money gambling and boozing it up in Las Vegas.

- Fearing that their retirement savings are inadequate, an unscrupulous couple in their fifties persuades the wife's elderly mother to transfer her Social Security checks to their personal account.

Whose stories are these?

About thirty individuals from all walks of life generously agreed to share their intensely personal stories with me. We spoke in person, on the phone, and via email. Most conversations lasted at least an hour and a half.

I found the people whose tales are featured in this book by word of mouth. Some contacted me through my blog, *Gold Diggers and Deadbeat Dads* at *ValerieRind.com*. Others reached out via social media such as Facebook, Twitter, and Google+. All I had to do was talk to anyone who would listen to me (and even those who wouldn't), and invariably they would say, "Oh, yes, that happened to my sister's friend Jane."

I also advertised on the Internet. You wouldn't believe how many people responded to a Craigslist ad under "Volunteers" with the heading "I want to interview you for a book I'm writing … if you've been scammed by a friend or relative."

Some individuals reached out and started sharing their stories, but later balked at telling more or meeting in person. I understood. I thought they were brave to respond at all.

I was amazed at how willing they all were to bare their souls and trust someone who was, in most cases, a total stranger. A few had never told anyone else about what had happened to them.

My volunteers became emotional when recounting their experiences. Talking about their past stirred up feelings of anger and sadness. They expressed disbelief that they "fell for it," that they made the same mistakes more than once, or that it took them so long to realize they had been conned. They were angry at the person who did them wrong, and even angrier at themselves. I understood their emotional reactions all too well.

Talking to me was a cathartic opportunity, as one woman said, "to get a little more bitterness off my chest." Another said she was relieved to discover that she wasn't "the only idiot on the planet."

All of the people I spoke with hoped that by publicly sharing their stories, they could reassure other people — perhaps you — that the world is full of silent victims of financial exploitation.

And most of all, those who revealed their past were eager to help prevent you from making similar blunders and experiencing the same financial fates.

I don't claim to be an investigative journalist. The objective wasn't to ferret out the absolute "truth." My sources told me only their sides of what are multi-faceted stories. The other players in their dramas no doubt have their own perspectives.

But I believe there is enormous value in discovering common themes and finding ways to avoid future downfalls.

Because I promised to respect their privacy, I changed all names, places, professions, and other identifying details to protect the innocent (and the guilty). Some conversations have been edited for clarity.

Yes, I am confident that their tales are true. You can't make this stuff up.

And, as painful as it is to admit, my stories are real as well.

At least nine categories

Each chapter in this book covers a different type of situation that can end in ruin, although there is plenty of overlap.

A thread that runs through many of the anecdotes is introduced in Chapter 1, *You Lied to Me*. Financial disaster often results when someone fibs or conceals important facts.

It was after I discovered the critical financial information that my husband had camouflaged for nearly a decade that I resolved to write this book.

Numerous people shared with me their compelling stories about spouses who lied by hiding mountains of credit card debt, drug addictions, or gambling problems. Some liars are so proficient at deception that psychology experts classify them as sociopaths.

Chapter 2, *I Loaned Money to You*, covers one of the most common transactions that goes wrong. A desperate borrower pressures the potential lender because of their close ties. The borrower may genuinely intend to repay the loan, but for some reason he never fully makes good on his promise. This chapter also includes considerations to take into account if you do decide to open a branch of YouBank — and what to do if you get stiffed.

Chapter 3, *I Co-signed for You and Got Sexually Transmitted Debt*[1], shows how you may be coerced to co-sign or guarantee a loved one's monetary obligations and wind up with your own finances in a shambles.

---

[1]   Sexually Transmitted Debt® is a registered trademark of VSJ Enterprises, LLC. This is the only footnote you will see in this book and there are no embedded hyperlinks in the text. For links and resources on specific topics, check the Resources section at the back of the book.

Often, a co-signer doesn't understand the full legal impact of signing her name on the line, or adding another person to her existing credit card account, particularly when that person turns out to be what I call a "Credit Cad."

A lot can go wrong when you rent an apartment with people you don't know too well.

Some slick operators enter relationships with ulterior economic motives. Chapter 4, *You're a Gold Digger,* showcases stories of men and women duped by partners who were more attracted to their financial assets than their personal qualities.

Chapter 5, *You Also Physically Abused Me,* deals with a particularly insidious type of perpetrator: abusive men who get others to take the financial fall for them. Their victims may be saddled with "coerced debt," a phenomenon that occurs at the tragic intersection of financial exploitation and domestic violence.

Chapter 6, *I Say 'I Do' to You, Your Assets, and Your Debts,* addresses commitment issues that may arise when two people get engaged or are seriously involved.

So you think you know your partner? Dig deeper — what else should you know? One man discovered his fiancée's financial foibles only when she moved in with him shortly before the wedding. If you live together before (or instead of) marriage, should you sign a cohabitation agreement? What about prenuptial and postnuptial agreements?

You're a Deadbeat Dad is about men who father one or more children but shirk their financial responsibility to support them. Chapter 7 shows how the mother and kids suffer, both economically and emotionally, when these cheapskates abandon them.

However, it's not just about negligent dads. I've also included a heartbreaking story of a heinous deadbeat mom.

Someone dies and before the body is buried, the question arises: Who gets what? Chapter 8, *Where There's a Will, There's a Relative*, looks at how to handle these tough situations. It also showcases second marriages where the blended family gets torn apart because of conflicting notions about entitlement to inheritances.

Chapter 9, *I've Got Grandma's Checkbook*, is about elder financial abuse, an epidemic that is often described as the crime of the twenty-first century. It happens when greedy friends or relatives take advantage of an older person by stealing money or valuable property from them.

For example, a manipulative adult convinces her aging mother to give her complete control of mom's finances. The daughter has easy access to the cash, yet there is little or no benefit for the senior. The other family members get stung if their sister grabs money that would have been part of their inheritances.

Heartless criminals commit unimaginable acts of physical and emotional abuse, even going as far as withholding food or medication until the elderly person complies with their demands. The victim may not even realize he or she is being financially bamboozled. If the senior citizen *can* see what is happening, he or she may be too scared or even unable to cry out for help.

Since the population in the U.S. is getting older — in fact, we are *all* getting older — Chapter 9 identifies the horrifying problem of elder financial abuse that will only get worse if we don't proactively address it.

Lastly, Chapter 10 offers *Ten Tips to Prevent Friends and Family From Ruining Your Finances.*

Everyone wants easy advice to keep them from making money mistakes like I did, right?

I can't offer you a magic preventative pill.

None of my advice in the final chapter is earthshattering new information. You've probably heard most of it many times before. I've just put it all in one place. You can find more detailed information from reputable personal finance bloggers and authors.

The final chapter shows that while there were few happy endings, most of the people who shared their stories with me found that life did go on. Things did get better. Many discovered personal strengths they didn't realize they had before their unfortunate experiences.

As for me, not only did I survive my own debacles, but I thrived. My experiences led to new careers in personal finance and writing.

I built a new life and gradually, a new life savings.

And I got to write this book!

Are they victims?

You may argue that people who were involved in financial transactions gone horribly wrong are not innocent victims. You may think I have no right to put myself and others in the same category as those who are the targets of physical abuse.

Some of the people I spoke with would agree with you. They admitted that on some level, they knew what was going on but chose to shut their eyes. Most harshly blamed themselves. I understand that is consistent with the reactions of abuse victims.

As you will see, I take plenty of responsibility for messing up my own life.

The one true exception is the financial mistreatment of our senior citizens. We cannot fault people whose physical and mental health is deteriorating while they become dependent on others for their personal care. They are genuine victims.

CHAPTER 1

You Lied to Me

My story: The ten-year lie

You've probably heard that money issues are among the top reasons people say they got divorced. In the end, my marriage became another casualty. My fault involved not asking the right questions; his was concealing critical information — or just plain lying.

I was the second Mrs. Mark. He was older than me by more than twenty years. When we dated, I knew nothing about what he owned or owed. I never asked and he didn't volunteer any information. The details didn't matter to me at the time.

Of course, it sounds like a total cliché: I married for love, not money.

Because of our age gap and Mark's apparent financial success, people pegged me as the quintessential young, gold diggin' gal. How ironic. Read my story in Chapter 2, *I Loaned Money to You*, to learn more about how I ended up nearly broke.

After our wedding, I moved into Mark's small, sparse condo, where he had lived for many years. I teased him that it was still decorated in 1970s bachelor-style.

A year later, we decided to rent a larger apartment. Mark suggested we keep the condo as an investment and rent it out. Our plan was to sell it and buy a house in a few years, after I'd finished law school and started working.

During my first year as an attorney, Mark lost his job at the architectural firm. He scoured the area for a new position, but it was difficult for a man in his fifties with his level of management experience to find something comparable. He decided to open his own company, working from home. We knew the first few years would be hard. Still, Mark assured me that a family of good, stable tenants had moved into the condo, and that their rent covered his mortgage payment and expenses.

Mark worked non-stop to get his business going. He reported that it generated income, albeit never enough to pay all the company's bills.

Our financial pressures got worse and our relationship became increasingly strained.

I had a few ideas. I suggested that Mark sell his tiny condo. He had nearly paid off the mortgage. The location was quite popular, particularly for young families. If he sold the condo, I reasoned, he could fund his business, repay the money I had "invested," and provide some cash for us to live on until we figured out what to do next. Perhaps we could move to an area with a lower cost of living.

But Mark refused to sell his home. He was adamant that it was important to him, for reasons he couldn't explain to me at first.

I knew that marriage is a partnership and sometimes you have to compromise. I reasoned that perhaps this was one of those times when, despite the five-figure debt he owed me, I should shut my mouth and respect his wishes.

Mark finally explained, "I want to keep the place so that when I die, I'll have something to leave to the kids [from his first marriage] and to you."

"I don't care about what I might inherit thirty years down the road," I snapped. "Instead, I'm worried about how we're going to pay the bills next month."

Still, he resisted.

I had another idea. We could move back into the condo. The mortgage payments were much less than the rent we paid for our larger apartment. It would be a bit cramped, but at least we'd have a roof over our heads and cheaper living expenses. He could also hang on to his sole financial asset.

When I asked Mark about the tenants, he confirmed that the same family still lived there. What about the lease — was it due to end anytime soon? If not, could we give the tenants some incentive to move out voluntarily? Mark said he'd check with his property manager. I became buried in my work and didn't ask Mark again about these possibilities. Yes, it was my fault for not following up.

Eventually I confided in my parents that I was unhappy in my marriage, and that we had major financial problems. I told them about Mark's resistance to do anything with the condo. Was I being unreasonable? Since keeping his old home meant so much to him, should I just drop it?

A dark cloud came over my father's face. He said, "Perhaps Mark can't sell it because he took a second mortgage or home equity loan to fund his business. Or perhaps he already sold the condo. You must check the city's real estate records to find out."

My dad was overreacting, I thought. How ridiculous! Of course Mark would have told me if he'd sold the condo! To satisfy my father, I went to examine the records in a musty office downtown, since they weren't available online.

I was flabbergasted.

My father was wrong.

Mark hadn't sold the condo or taken a second mortgage.

He'd never owned it. Let me repeat: *Mark had never owned the condo.*

Without realizing it, I'd lived in a rented apartment at the beginning of our marriage. And for the next eight years, I'd continued to believe that condo was his property and a critical part of our financial future.

Whenever I had asked Mark about the tenants, he'd told me it was an Asian family. The truth was that a Japanese couple had owned the condo for many years. Mark was only a tenant. I'm sure he never added my name to the lease.

I felt devastated that I had been so clueless.

Now it all made sense why Mark refused to sell or move back into the condo. As I'd learned in my first-year Property Law class, if you don't own it, you can't sell it. *Nemo dat quod non habet,* as they say in Latin.

Game over. I couldn't stay married to a man who had lied to my face for a decade. And I'm just giving you the top story here; you'll learn more about my situation in Chapter 2, *I Loaned Money to You.*

What would you do next?

When I first discovered his deception, I didn't confront Mark. I didn't say a word, even though I felt like my whole body was going to explode. Or implode. But I had no idea how he would react. He had never laid a hand on me. However, he had a bit of a temper, and I had uncovered one of his dark personal failures.

I formulated an exit strategy to get out of the marriage while minimizing the risk of incurring Mark's possible wrath. The first steps were consulting a divorce attorney and searching for a new home. It was difficult to secure a new lease, because I discovered that Mark was behind on paying our rent.

Now it was *my* turn to be a liar. I found it exhausting — it took so much emotional energy to keep all the details straight! I stuck to my usual routine while concocting cover stories with plausible answers to any possible questions. For once, I had to be one big step ahead of Mark.

For example, one Saturday while I looked at apartments, I mentioned to Mark that my friend Amy and I were visiting the art museum. I told Amy the plan and researched the current exhibition so that I could talk about it if Mark asked.

On the days I normally went swimming at the health club, I stopped by for a quick dip in the pool so that I returned home as usual, smelling faintly of chlorine and carrying a damp towel.

How did anyone live like this on a regular basis?

I moved out surreptitiously a few weeks later when Mark was away. It was one of the hardest things I've ever had to do. The phone call was excruciating.

"Mark, I've … I'm … I'm leaving. I moved out of the apartment. It's over."

He gasped. "What? Why? Have you already signed a lease?"

Mark didn't take it well. He was furious with me; he didn't like having the entire living room carpet pulled out from beneath him. Yet he tried hard to convince me to come back.

I refused.

All I wanted to know was *why* Mark had lied to me for all those years. Why did he go to such elaborate lengths to conceal the truth? How long did Mark think he could get away with his charade?

Mark admitted to being embarrassed that he was in his early fifties and had nothing material to show for it. He rented a small apartment, owned no real estate, drove a company car, and had only a corporate credit card. So when we started dating, he simply told me he owned the condo.

This made me even angrier than the fact that he had lied.

"If you thought when we met that I cared whether you owned that damn condo, then you didn't know me at all. And you don't know me now!" I cried.

Sure, I like having nice things. Who doesn't? But I was insulted and hurt that Mark had pegged me as being so shallow that I wouldn't have married him if I knew the truth.

Mark abused my trust when he lied about something so fundamental.

My friends and family reassured me that Mark's financial deception was driven by how he felt about himself rather than what he thought about me.

You may say I bailed without even trying to save our marriage. However, you can't imagine how I felt when I examined those real estate records in stark black and white. It was a colossal "Ah ha!" moment. Or more an overwhelming "Oh no!" moment, like I had been sucker-punched.

Perhaps it's like finding your spouse having sex with a stranger in your own bed. Some couples overcome that type of betrayal, work things out, and stay together.

Not me. Even if we patched things up somehow, I would always doubt whatever Mark told me about financial matters. I could no longer trust him. That's not my idea of marriage.

To this day, I still have no idea why Mark owned nothing of any value. Nor do I know how much credit card or other debt he had. My huge fumble was that I never asked him any questions about his financial position, either before or after we married. Perhaps he had filed for bankruptcy before I appeared on the scene. Whatever happened, he expertly concealed it. I never found out. And in the long run, it doesn't matter.

Recently I checked the real estate records for that condo. They were online, so I didn't have to trudge to the dusty, musty office downtown. It took only a few minutes to find out that the same Japanese couple still owned it. They'd bought the property from the original developer more than thirty years ago — long before I met Mark.

My ex-husband later understood his mistake, in his own way. About a year after we separated, Mark sent me a short note. He said he'd told me the only thing that he thought would win me, but in the end it was exactly why he lost me.

Mark was so wrong about the first part. The second part? He was spot-on correct.

Jenny's story: Separate lives, separate accounts

I met with Jenny, who is a lively, articulate woman in her early sixties, on a dreary winter afternoon. She told me she was unaware on her wedding day that her groom was a raging alcoholic. Louis was in the military and was periodically stationed overseas. Jenny lived stateside with their son. She worked full time as a government analyst and deposited her whole paycheck in their joint checking account. Louis handled all their accounts and bills electronically from afar.

Jenny had no idea that her husband was secretly siphoning off part of his paycheck.

"I never imagined he could put money in a separate account," this intelligent woman told me. She doesn't know where all the money went; Jenny suspects he drank most of it. In addition, Louis was writing bad checks on their joint account. He eventually gave Jenny the bill-paying duties, but without first telling his wife about the sorry state of their financial affairs.

The bank started calling because all her checks were bouncing. Creditors pursued her about overdue bills for charges she didn't recognize. Jenny was shocked when she realized Louis had run up the debt while overseas. It took her months to straighten out the whole mess.

Jenny's initial error was quite simple: she didn't know how much her spouse earned. It's not uncommon. Personal income is an uncomfortable topic for many people, especially if their self-worth is tied to a salary figure. However, domestic partners have a right to know. If you don't know how much is available in the money bucket, how can you budget for daily expenditures or plan for long-term expenses? It's like shopping blind — you don't know how much you can spend or what your credit limit is.

Louis didn't share with his wife the details of his compensation, so she had no way of knowing that part of his net pay was being funneled into his private account.

There's nothing wrong with having a checking or savings account in your own name; in fact, I believe it is a good arrangement for any committed couple. However, it may be a warning sign if you find out that your spouse is stashing away large amounts of cash.

Jenny shared her story with me many years after their divorce. She was still furious that Louis was a liar and had left their finances in a shambles. I think she'll carry that anger forever.

George's story: *"The lying is worse than the spending"*

Twenty years ago, just before George married Carlita, she confessed she was more than $28,000 in debt. It didn't take him long to see why. Carlita worked, but she also loved shopping, giving lavish gifts, and having fancy lunches with her girlfriends.

After they married, she routinely ran up big credit card bills — and George paid them. He got angry, but Carlita blamed him for not earning enough money to support her spending habit. Their marriage counselor pointed out that increasing his salary wasn't the solution, because she would ramp up her spending to match his higher income. Carlita didn't want to hear it. She continued to zealously charge up a storm.

For his part, George was also unfaithful in his marriage, with respect to his finances. He surreptitiously searched Carlita's wallet for additional credit cards. George checked their mail and shredded any offers for new credit that were addressed to his wife. He even resorted to hiding some of his income in other bank accounts.

After several months of subterfuge on George's part, the situation seemed to improve. Carlita was not incurring mountains of debt and the inflow of new credit seemed to have eased. However, George uncovered a much bigger problem quite by accident. He explained it to me via email:

> I now know why she wasn't running up credit card debt. It seems she dipped into the money that we agreed to put away for our son's college education. I guesstimate I have to make up somewhere

in the neighborhood of $57,000. You'd think I'd be upset by all this, but I am not. I guess I am sort of more hurt that she lied, more than that she spent the money ... I don't think I am mad or sad. I am just kind of numb. I suspect people feel this way when their spouse is on drugs or is an alcoholic.

George learned about the missing money when he tried to transfer funds to an investment account in an effort to get a better return on their savings.

How would you react?

George remained calm and didn't yell when he confronted Carlita. "She kept telling me she wanted to talk it out," he told me, "but my view is that any talking that needed to be done had already been done. What is there to say when trust is betrayed again and again?"

Whenever George asked her why she didn't tell him about the missing money or her continuous shopping binges, Carlita said that she didn't want him to get upset. He sarcastically pointed out to me the fallacy of this logic: "Of course, I'll be less upset when I find out I have been lied to on top of the wild spending!"

I understood exactly how George felt. As I explained in my story of my husband's ten-year fib, the dishonesty was worse than the economic facts.

George acknowledged his role in this mess and the effect it has had on his life:

I have been an enabler for my wife. I have covered the debts for years. I am getting burnt out and my health is starting to suffer. I am so tired of struggling with this insanity. But I love my wife. Carlita is not a monster. She is a good mother and a nice person. It's just this damn issue with her spending. I just don't understand this kind of behavior. For the life of me, I don't!

George got infected with a whopping case of Sexually Transmitted Debt when his wife concealed her huge credit card charges on their joint accounts (for more, see Chapter 3, *I Co-signed for You and Got Sexually Transmitted Debt*). Carlita was financially unfaithful when she misappropriated their assets by draining the college savings. George contributed to their bad situation by hiding money and intercepting her credit card offers.

George's solution was not to divorce his wife, but to divorce his finances from hers. They split the household bills, but she has no access to the savings accounts.

He is determined to find some way to make up the missing college funds. George swore to me that he will never tell their son how his own mother stole his educational future.

Elise's story: "Why didn't I see it?"

Imagine if you discovered after being married for a few years that your husband had an insatiable appetite for betting on the horses and snorting cocaine. Elise shared with me her tale of woe during our long phone conversation.

Elise and Jon were in their early thirties when they met, fell in love, and soon got engaged. Easygoing and fun to be around, Jon told Elise he made a decent living working for his father's vending machine business. Elise's boss met her fiancé only once and said: "You can't marry that man. He's no good for you." Elise wasn't interested in her supervisor's personal appraisal, and she ignored the warning.

As a buyer for an upscale clothing store, Elise had a lucrative and exciting career. However, she struggled with working long hours. Jon encouraged her to quit and told her he'd take care of her. At first, Elise balked at the idea. This was her career, not just a job, and she had worked long and hard to get to her current position. But it became even more difficult, so she resigned.

Not long after, she discovered the true cause of her malaise: Elise was pregnant.

Their son Scott was born when Elise was thirty-three years old. Transitioning to full-time motherhood was difficult. She struggled with being alone all day with a baby and she worried about her parenting abilities. On top of that, Jon started disappearing for hours at a time without telling Elise where he was going or what he would be doing. When confronted, he always had some work-related excuse. Jon's stories seemed a bit lame to Elise, but he always had a believable explanation when she questioned him closely.

At her husband's suggestion, Elise gave Jon the responsibilities of keeping their bank accounts and paying the household bills.

Uh oh — start the movie soundtrack that tells you something bad is going to happen.

Elise's father gave the couple a generous gift of $25,000 toward a down payment on a house. She assumed that Jon deposited the check in their joint savings account, but in fact, he gambled all the money away at the racetrack. Every penny. He had been convinced he could double their money, but he lost far more. He continued to pick the wrong horses in desperate attempts to win big and replace his father-in-law's gift and feed his growing cocaine habit.

Jon also stole money from his own father's company. His father stopped speaking to Jon and blamed Elise for the couple's situation. Why? The way Jon's father saw it, Elise came from a wealthy family and expected that her husband would support her in that lifestyle, even if he couldn't afford it.

Without telling Elise, Jon visited her older brother, Duncan, and pleaded for a $12,000 loan. He told Duncan that his bookies were threatening to kill Elise and their son, Scott, if Jon didn't pay his debts in a few days. Jon showed Duncan the gun he carried because he feared for their lives.

Duncan didn't have a lot of money, but he would do anything to keep his little sister and nephew safe. He gave Jon $12,000, but didn't tell Elise because he wanted to "protect" her. For several years, Elise's entire family shielded her from the truth that her husband was addicted to gambling and drugs.

The IRS sent them notices about unpaid back taxes. Elise didn't understand and she couldn't get a straight answer from her husband. She was harassed by phone calls from banks and collection companies about overdue payments. It didn't make sense; she thought that Jon paid all their bills.

Angry people called and yelled that Jon owed them money. They promised to hurt her and Scott if Jon didn't pay the $5,000 or $10,000 they'd loaned him. Elise didn't know any of these people, and she was frightened and unnerved by their menacing calls.

Elise felt as though she was nearing a breakdown, so she reached out to her brother for help. Duncan investigated and was outraged to discover that all the credit cards were maxed out. Elise and Jon were in debt to the tune of more than $120,000. At this point, Duncan finally told his sister about Jon's addictions. Elise was furious that her whole family had hidden the truth from her.

The couple filed for bankruptcy. Elise described her experience to me:

> It was creepy. You go in this room and hear all these other people's stories. This wasn't what I grew up with — I was raised with the values of integrity, honor, and honesty. This was dark and dirty.

It was Jon's idea for them to move across the country. He thought the timing was right because his bookie was in jail.

Wasn't it time to dump him? Why did Elise stay with Jon?

"I was scared," Elise explained to me. "I'd gained a lot of weight during the pregnancy that I hadn't yet shed, and I was afraid that no other man would think I was attractive. And I really didn't want to be an unemployed single mom with a four-year-old child."

She convinced herself that she and her husband had pledged to stay together in sickness and in health, and that his gambling and drug dependencies were curable illnesses. Elise and Scott went with Jon, on the condition that he get help with his problems. Jon swore that he would.

Of course, Jon didn't get help. He went to therapy but was not serious about the process.

Jon began to hang out with the local seedy characters. Always outgoing and charming, he made friends easily but was quick to alienate them. Elise was suspicious of Jon's close relationship with his female boss. People told her he was sleeping around. She saw on his computer that he visited porn websites. A woman accused Jon of rape, although he wasn't arrested.

Elise's regular therapist met him once and told her that Jon had a criminal mind. He would never change, and she must leave immediately. She didn't.

The (almost) final straw came when Elise found a large quantity of cocaine in their apartment. But around the same time, her stepmother was diagnosed with leukemia and given only a few months to live. Elise wanted Jon to stay with her and help take care of Scott. Another woman claimed that she was sleeping with Jon, but all Elise could think about was her stepmother's terminal illness. After her death, the couple stayed together until Jon said he wanted to separate for a few weeks.

Elise gathered her strength, filed for divorce, and told Jon he couldn't come home. He didn't fight her for custody of Scott.

It was no surprise when Jon became the quintessential deadbeat dad.

Like many of the people who told me stories about their lying spouses, Elise said: "Why didn't I see it?"

She did admit that on some level, she knew Jon was involved in betting and doing drugs. However, it was too hard for her to deal with the whole situation at the time. Elise wasn't able to acknowledge that her relationship with Jon was toxic until she was ready to function as a single mom.

It's best not to beat yourself up too much for past mistakes. We move on when we're ready.

Briana's story: "He was a gambler but claimed I was an embezzler"

Briana acknowledges that there are two sides to the story when a marriage fails. "In my world, I'm always right," she told me during a late-night phone conversation. "In his view — I ran our business into the ground."

I asked Briana what she knew about David's finances before they married. Had she asked him about his debt or savings?

She admitted, "I didn't know much. I guess he lived paycheck to paycheck. Because David came from a poor family, I was pleased at how far he had come and how well he had done for himself."

Briana didn't question him about his financial situation, even though she knew David and his ex-wife had divorced because of vague money issues that he never explained. He dutifully paid child support; David was no deadbeat dad. He also supported a daughter he'd had out of wedlock, although there was always drama with that baby mama.

Briana and David met and fell in love when they were co-workers at a large international technology corporation in the Boston area. The company closed their division but offered them comparable jobs in New Jersey. Briana would have been happy to relocate, because they were both relatively senior at this stable company and received decent paychecks and benefits.

But David's dream was to stay in Boston and start a technology consulting business. Briana agreed to go along with the plan. They collected healthy severance packages and used that money to fund the new venture and cover some of their living expenses during the startup phase.

When her dad passed away, Briana inherited close to $100,000. She spent most of the money converting their attic into an office and buying computer equipment. The business paid rent to her for the office space. David paid for their living expenses while they built the business. By the fourth year of operations, their company was doing quite well.

However, like many small ventures operating out of attics, basements, and garages, they got caught when the economy tanked. Their business income plummeted. Briana took on temporary secretarial work in addition to continuing the day-to-day work of their company.

David traveled frequently, often to Europe. Briana was stuck at home minding the consulting business, working at her day job, and looking after their two daughters. It was a stressful time; one of the girls had a serious sports injury and the other nearly flunked out of college.

When David returned home from overseas trips, he whined and complained that Briana didn't spend enough time with him. He acted like a bratty child.

She told me, "He needed a lot of personal attention and got angry when I didn't have any energy left for him at the end of each long day."

The couple tried marriage counseling, but David's hectic travel schedule and Briana's concerns about the kids made it easy for them to brush all the difficult marital issues aside. Often they didn't follow up on their counseling assignments, or even go to the appointments.

Briana and David were stuck on an emotional treadmill where things would flare up and then settle down. David declared that he wanted a divorce. Briana agreed, but they never pursued it. Neither one spoke with a lawyer.

They treated the divorce issue almost as if no one remembered to pick up the shirts at the dry cleaner.

David became more distant and paranoid. "He accused me of having affairs while he was away," Briana told me. "Once I met up with my brother at a conference in Philadelphia. David got it in his head that I was sleeping with my brother's work colleagues. Of course, I wasn't. But he was distrustful and didn't believe me."

He hacked into her Facebook account and saw messages from a college boyfriend. They were catching up on each other's lives and had no intention of meeting in person, yet somehow David became convinced that a clandestine rendezvous was in the works.

(As an aside: Why are so many of the characters in these stories able to handily break into their spouse's email or Facebook accounts? Doesn't anyone heed the warnings about having strong passwords and not divulging them to *anyone*?)

Briana didn't realize it at the time, but David was an example straight out of a Psychology 101 textbook — he was projecting his own bad behavior onto her. It wasn't until much later that she uncovered all of his lies and secrets.

Briana said, "I found out that he had online gambling accounts. David gave the feeble excuse that he had the accounts because his *friend* didn't want them. I didn't buy it."

David was stingy with gifts. For their anniversary, he offered her a two-night stay at a casino in Atlantic City. Briana didn't like gambling, so it was a pathetic gesture. She tagged along, trying to keep the peace. But David disappeared for hours and didn't return to their hotel room. Disgusted, Briana gave up and went home alone.

David became more suspicious and accused Briana of stealing money from their consulting business. Briana knew it was high time to file for divorce.

Briana's divorce lawyer asked David's attorney to provide David's bank account statements for the past three years — standard procedure during a divorce. When they didn't hand over the documents as requested, Briana's lawyer subpoenaed five years of financial records.

Boxes of documents were delivered to Briana. She was perplexed when she examined the statements. "It took me three hours to review all the papers. I tried to make sense of it. I really didn't want to believe what I saw."

What did she find?

"I almost threw up. Not only had he subscribed to numerous online dating sites for the past five years, but he had also been gambling at race tracks and casinos."

In one year, David withdrew more than $62,000 from ATMs located in casinos — and this amount didn't include money that he got from other ATMs and banks.

The records showed that David made lots of cash withdrawals at the same casino in a single day. People don't normally stop by a casino just to use an ATM, so it's a safe bet that David lost the money that the machine tirelessly ejected at the blackjack tables.

All the cash in their joint savings account and most of David's retirement funds were gone. Briana estimates that a total of $200,000 vanished over five years — not including money he took from the overdraft account, his personal line of credit, and cash advances on credit cards.

"I thought we were struggling like most normal families. We could glimpse the end of the tunnel in four years when our youngest daughter would graduate from college." Telling me this part of her story, Briana sighed, "Even my lawyer didn't expect things to be *this* bad."

Their respective attorneys sent the couple to divorce mediation. For Briana, it would be risky to appear before a judge who might classify gambling as a mere financial risk that David took, almost like a bad investment. The couple made a deal: Briana wouldn't attack him for his gambling losses if David didn't try to grab her retirement account. It wasn't an equal trade, but she and her attorney thought she had too much to lose if the judge ruled that the gambling losses were no big deal.

The mediator required the couple to continue living under the same roof because they didn't earn enough money to maintain two households. Can you imagine going through a divorce and being forced to stay together?

Their accountant emailed Briana and asked if she had completed the payroll taxes yet for their company. David saw the email and was furious. He decided that she was mismanaging the business. Briana claims that the taxes were not even due yet.

David accused Briana of drawing a salary from their business without doing anything while working at her temp job outside the home. He also claimed she owed him for taxes and her use of the corporate credit card.

One night when Briana came home, she found papers that David placed on the bed. He had written up formal invoices for $80,000 and $47,000 for her alleged failures to reimburse the business for personal expenses.

Trying to get cash from her wasn't enough for David. He went first to the County Prosecutor and then to the State Attorney's Office in an attempt to get Briana charged with embezzlement. They laughed at him; he presented no concrete evidence and his "invoices" were based on what he perceived she owed. Even both divorce attorneys agreed that she hadn't misused the company's funds.

Because David emptied the funds in his 401(k) account before he reached retirement age, they owed taxes and penalties. The couple had to sell their home just to pay their IRS tab and legal fees. In the end, Briana ended up with about $70,000. The business they'd started together no longer had any economic value.

With a deep sigh, she said to me, "Money is a huge issue, but I'll be OK in the long run. Thankfully, I have a terrific family. My brother is my eldest daughter's godfather and pays her college tuition and rent. My other brother helped me buy a townhouse. Instead of paying rent, I pay him the interest on the mortgage. We are joint owners of the property and signed a promissory note. There are no family secrets. My daughters know all about this arrangement."

Briana was embarrassed about being divorced. She said she felt like a complete failure. "It's mortifying to be starting over at fifty years old. I had a great career and then my own business. Now all I have is a low-paying job with no heath insurance or benefits." David is required to pay her a small amount of spousal support, about $450 per month for the next four years.

Despite all the signs, David has never admitted that he has a gambling problem. He still claims that he didn't cheat on his wife.

"It's the end of a dream. So sad," she lamented. "But he is not the person I married. It's disgusting to think about all the awful things he did. I don't know how I'll ever trust again."

She concluded, "You can't allow someone to destroy your financial future, like mine was destroyed. But I am extremely blessed and fortunate to have family and friends who are so supportive, both financially and emotionally."

She often tells herself, "This too shall pass."

Why lie?

Money is perhaps the most personal, controversial, and taboo topic of non-conversation. Most people would rather tell their friends about their sex life than reveal the amount of their salary, debt, or bank account balance. Instead of being honest and upfront, it's often easier to avoid the subject, or to tell a little silvery lie.

True or False? Survey says...

What do we share with those who are closest to us — our significant others? Surveys on the topic of financial infidelity all indicate that domestic dishonesty about money is not unusual.

One survey conducted in 2012 by TODAY.com and *SELF* magazine of more than 23,000 adults revealed that 37 percent of men and 56 percent of women admitted to fibbing to their partner about money, mostly about spending. Meanwhile, the AARP Bulletin Survey on Financial Honesty conducted in 2012 found that 34 percent of respondents had concealed purchases from their partner.

A January 2014 study of couples with combined finances by The Harris Poll on behalf of the National Endowment for Financial Education showed similar statistics. One out of three adults admitted to some form of financial infidelity, including hiding purchases, cash, bills, or statements.

While financial fudging seems commonplace, this latest study also found that 35 percent of respondents felt they *should* have the right to keep aspects of their finances confidential, even from their spouses.

Of course, you have to wonder about how reliable these statistics are. The reality could be much worse.

After all, why would people tell the complete truth when answering an online survey — about dishonesty?

Why do we do this? Why do so many people find it necessary to hide their latest iGadget or new pair of shoes, as if they were having an intimate affair with their Christian Louboutin® pumps? The *SELF* magazine and TODAY.com survey mentioned in the box above found that people kept money secrets because they didn't agree with their spouses about spending.

Cash issues are so personal.

Most of us aren't aware of our feelings about financial matters. For some, spending money is an exhilarating pleasure; for others, pulling out their wallet is a painful ordeal. One man is terrified of having any debt, while his friend is not overly concerned about owing thousands of dollars, or even filing for bankruptcy. Money hoarders worry that they will never amass "enough," while spendthrifts are confident that they can always score more cash.

To some degree, we are a product of our monetary upbringing. We either act as our parents did, or we make a conscious effort to behave differently. Growing up in a frugal household may instill in us good economic habits for life. Or instead, we may spend with gusto to acquire the things we never had.

Years ago, I saw a TV commercial featuring a man standing proudly in the doorway of his first new house. He took great pleasure in opening the front door wide and letting all the heat out — in defiance of his father's strict rule against wasting money on the heating bill for his childhood home.

Do opposite money "personalities" attract or repel? When you unite two people with different attitudes, experiences, approaches, and feelings about money, conflicts can arise.

Couples may consist of a spender and a saver. If one partner insists on buying a new car every two years but the other will book a vacation only at the absolute cheapest motel, the war is on. It's a failure to agree on the financial ground rules at home. And sometimes the easiest way to prevent these battles is to lie.

How do you know if a lover or partner is camouflaging a financial fact? It may be difficult to tell. An expert concealer can keep it undercover for a long time, perhaps forever.

In my case, it was a decade before I stumbled upon the truth that my husband didn't own the home we'd lived in.

A person hiding the truth may simply omit a financial fact, such as not divulging the price of a novelty item that she impulsively bought on eBay. Or, in a worst-case scenario, you may be involved with someone whose prevarication is so habitual and destructive that it's pathological behavior.

Uncovering facts before commitment

If your relationship is getting "serious" (however you define it), you owe it to yourself to do some due diligence on your lover before you make a major life decision. Read Chapter 6, *I Say 'I Do' to You, Your Assets, and Your Debts,* for more on the financial facts you should know.

Here is a short recap. Find out if your partner has:

- A lot of debt (although it's subjective how much "a lot" is)

- A past bankruptcy (or two)

- A history of financial irresponsibility (repeated failures to pay rent or bills on time)

- An obligation to pay alimony or child support

- A pending lawsuit that could wipe him out if it ends badly

- A platoon of collection agencies chasing her.

A "yes" answer is not, by itself, an automatic reason to end your relationship. However, you need to have some idea of what you're getting yourself into, because your partner's economic past will directly affect your financial future.

You can glean information from credit reports, bank statements, and income tax returns — provided the other person has consented. Of course, it's only fair that you open your own kimono and disclose your numbers in return.

If anything seems vague or inconsistent, ask questions. Always trust your gut feeling. There's no guarantee you'll find out everything you need to know, or that your sweetheart won't cover up something later. Just find out whatever you can and discuss it together.

Oh, how I wish I had been smart enough to investigate before I married Mark.

Lying after commitment

What if you're already married and you suspect your partner is keeping a critical monetary detail from you? Unless you're being unreasonably paranoid, you may be correct.

Look for certain clues:

- He is evasive about certain bills, bank statements, or other mail

- Her phone rings often with urgent calls or texts from people you don't know

- You're asked to sign papers without adequate explanations

- When you ask about money matters, you get dodgy answers

- He or she is often inexplicably late, absent, or unavailable.

It's as if your partner is having a sexual affair — sometimes you just know it.

I found out you lied to me

Many people who talked with me reacted the same way as I did when they discovered that their partners or close family members had hidden financial facts.

We were far more upset about being lied to than about any actual monetary loss. The betrayal cut so deeply. We put our complete trust in someone who took full fiscal advantage of us. Ouch. Exploitation hurts.

So what do you do when you find out your partner bamboozled, tricked, or deceived you?

I can't give you a one-size-fits-all answer. It depends on your personal circumstances and the severity of the infidelity. Below I offer you some general guidelines.

Please keep in mind that it may be wise for you to consult a professional, such as a therapist, before taking any action.

First, consider why your partner may have lied. What was his or her motive for fudging the household bottom line?

Surveys consistently show that people often fib to their partners — most commonly about spending — to avoid criticism and conflict.

Can you and your partner find a compromise to better align your spending habits? Perhaps you can agree that each person is entitled to spend a set amount of cash each month however they want, with no questions asked and no disapproval.

What if you discover a major deception? She forged your signature. He maxed out all the credit cards. Large sums of cash are gone. Your house is in foreclosure.

Now you are in much trickier territory. I believe that ultimately you do need to confront the culprit. If you bury the fact that you know about the lies, you are adding another dimension of deceit to your relationship.

It's true that I lied to Mark about a lot of things for a few weeks, while I plotted my getaway. It was unpleasant and stressful. However, I felt that telling some untruths was necessary to ensure my physical and emotional safety. I also wanted to avoid getting talked into staying with him if I had a moment of weakness.

Please consider how to approach your partner with your fiscal discovery. Experts on the psychology of lying agree that certain liars are subconsciously ruled by their feelings of personal inadequacy. If you blow their cover, you hit them in their soft underbelly of perceived failures. And you have no idea how they'll react.

Take a deep breath, calm down, and check your facts. Could there be an innocent explanation? Perhaps the funds were not depleted, but were moved to another account or type of investment to earn a better return. Credit card statements list the merchants, so you can see where she was shopping. Maybe your wife bought you a surprise birthday present.

When you are reasonably sure that there is no "good" explanation, it's time to confront your partner. Easier said than done — I'll be the first to admit it. Emailing or texting is not appropriate, nor is calling someone at work. It may be best to discuss the issue in person. In some circumstances, this conversation should happen only when an objective, neutral third person, such as a counselor, is present.

The only way I felt safe was calling Mark on the phone after I relocated to my new apartment. To tell my husband I was never coming home was agonizing; it was the worst call I've ever had to make. I still remember the phone being slippery because my hand was sweating so much. But I thought he deserved to hear this devastating news from me in real time, rather than reading a "Dear Mark" letter or walking into the half-emptied apartment.

Be prepared for the initial reaction. Because you stumbled upon the truth, your partner will probably be angry with you for snooping. Your investigation may have been justified, but in the ideal partnership there would be no significant financial surprises. Try not to let an irate initial response deflect you from the discussions you need to have.

See if your partner can explain *why* he or she felt the need to distort the truth. Try to avoid blame and accusations.

Instead, express your concerns about both how your discovery affects you personally and what it may mean for the household finances.

Next, discuss how the two of you will handle the fiscal problem; for example, determine a reasonable plan to pay off the credit card debt.

Look for ways to improve communication. Perhaps you could hold an informal State of Our Financial Union meeting each month or quarter to set and review your goals and calculate the money coming in and going out. Your ultimate goal is to achieve economic stability and harmony at home.

None of this is easy or happens overnight, even in the best of relationships.

Cleaning up a mess may be easier if an impartial person takes an active role in your recovery. Consider hiring a financial planner or reputable credit counselor to help both of you handle your monetary moves so there's no repeat performance. You may also want to consider going to a professional therapist for couples counseling.

Lying as an extreme sport

Social psychologist Robert Feldman contends that most people routinely engage in what he calls "cosmetic deceit" to make themselves appear better than they are. We all have our own ideas about what "better" is and how to position and showcase ourselves to others.

The tipping point is what you are willing to do to project the best picture.

There's a world of difference between doctoring the household checkbook balance and having a full-time *modus operandi* of dishonesty.

The obvious question, of course, is how do you steer clear of getting involved with a pathological liar?

If you have never been ensnared by a master of deceit with a talent for spin, they're impossible to spot. Especially when you're madly in love. Always slick and charming, they are experts at telling you what you want to hear. Crafty chameleons become whatever you need them to be. The more emotionally involved you are, the more you trust and believe them. You don't have any reason to doubt what they tell you about money or anything else. These smooth talkers will always have a quick and plausible answer to your questions.

Pathological liars just keep getting better at deceiving you while appearing to be genuine.

My ex-husband Mark engaged in his elaborate charade for years because he didn't trust that I would accept him for who he was, based solely on what material things he owned. I don't think he's an evil person, but he was a skilled con artist. All for no good reason.

Susan Forward, Ph.D., therapist and author of *When Your Lover is a Liar: Healing the Wounds of Deception and Betrayal*, argues that certain men who lie are incurable sociopaths. She claims that millions of educated and savvy women fall victim to charming, seductive manipulators who have an uncanny talent to trap and exploit them. These extreme liars have a "disease of the conscience" and are incapable of change, claims Dr. Forward.

She offers a laundry list of behavioral traits to look out for, such as being glib, persuasive, impulsive, unfaithful, and easily bored. These men (and women!) blame others for their own failures. When caught lying, they promise not to do it again, and if you question them too closely, they react by accusing *you* of being untrusting and not loving them.

Don't push them into individual or couples counseling, cautions Dr. Forward, who believes that therapy is a total waste of time for sociopathic liars. They truly believe they're not wrong, feel no guilt about their actions, and attend counseling only because they have to — and of course, they won't tell the truth to their partner or the therapist.

Do the characteristics above sound familiar to you? If so, Dr. Forward advises, leave. Immediately, and with extreme caution.

Elise's portrayal of her husband, who hid his gambling and drug problems, fits the profile. Here's how she described Jon to me:

> He was funny and outgoing. Not too intelligent, but smart enough. Jon had charisma — he got people pulled into his web. He would fake people out to get what he needed until they found out. He always said to me, 'I'm sorry, I really love you, I screwed up, I can't live without you.'

Fortunately, Elise was able to extricate herself and her son from Jon's lies and his dangerous addictions.

Conclusions

Ask questions and trust your gut instinct. If you get answers that sound plausible but don't feel quite right, poke around a little more. Keep in mind that most people are uncomfortable talking about money, particularly if they made big mistakes in the past that ended in misfortune.

If you suspect you've been deceived by a significant other or family member:

- Check the facts before you make assumptions and accusations.

- Calm down before you confront them.

- Consider consulting a therapist together.

- Accept that if your partner is a compulsive, sociopathic liar, he or she may never change.

- Decide what your next course of action is — will you stay or will you go?

- Seek help for yourself from a professional counselor.

CHAPTER 2

I Loaned Money to You

Does this sound familiar? It's a classic pattern of financial exploitation: Your friend or lover borrows money but before they pay you back, they ask for more. You, as the lender, have difficulty saying no. Due to your close ties, the manipulative borrower knows what buttons to push to get the cash he wants from his unsuspecting financier. In an intimate relationship, you trust your partner and you want to demonstrate your love. You may worry that if you balk, the borrower will leave you.

Empty Accountitis

It's another monetary malady. You got involved with someone and lent them money. You were sure they'd pay you back. The next thing you know, you've been taken to the financial cleaners. Nothing left in the bank.

You've got Empty Accountitis.

Read almost any chapter in this book and you'll see lots of ways to end up with a zero balance when you let friends and relatives ooze into your economic life.

My story: I was a smart lawyer, but a stupid wife

I never thought it could happen to me. How did my loving husband cheat me out of my life savings? How did I get infected with Sexually Transmitted Debt?

In my thirties, I was happily married and employed as a commercial attorney in a large law firm. My husband Mark worked as a manager at an architectural firm. Suddenly he lost his job. He couldn't find a comparable position, so he decided to start his own business. Mark said he would use his own savings to fund this venture. I never asked him how much money he had to invest, or what he planned to do if it ran out.

MISTAKE #1: I was ignorant about my husband's financial affairs. I just didn't think to ask about his bank balance. Or his debts. Money is a taboo subject, even between partners. Please read Chapter 6, *I Say 'I Do' to You, Your Assets, and Your Debts,* which suggests the kinds of things I think you might want to know before you marry or seriously commit to someone.

One day, Mark asked if I would loan his business about $15,000 because of a short-term cash flow problem. I was happy to help, especially because my husband had supported me for three years while I was in law school.

MISTAKE #2: I didn't ask any questions about how he got into this jam. I even agreed with him that the bank was being unreasonable by demanding a deposit that same day. Warning bells should have been clanging in my ears, because debt problems do not materialize overnight. Later I found out the truth; Mark had been having trouble paying his bills for quite a few months.

Meanwhile, back at the law firm, I was managing large commercial transactions. Every day I negotiated complex international contracts involving hundreds of millions of dollars. Smart Attorney Valerie would have required Mark to sign something saying he owed me money, with a promise to repay within a definite time frame. Yet at home, I was thinking like Good Wife Valerie instead of thinking like a lawyer.

MISTAKE #3 was not asking Mark to sign an IOU. I had every reason to trust my husband, right?

A week after he asked for $15,000, Mark asked for $2,000 more. No problem. A few months later, another $5,000. OK, whatever you need, darling. One day he asked for $25,000. Almost all I had left to my name was a $30,000 certificate of deposit. We agreed that I would cash in the CD, deposit the entire $30,000 in his business account, and then he would immediately transfer the extra $5,000 back to me. Mark promised that soon he would repay the $25,000, as well as the $22,000 he had already borrowed.

Mark didn't transfer the $5,000 back to my account.

I finally asked Mark to write a note acknowledging that his company had borrowed all this money from me. I felt uncomfortable asking, because it looked like I didn't trust him. Why didn't I expect my husband to keep his financial vows? He was the man I loved. I'd married him for richer and for poorer, right?

Mark agreed to sign an IOU. He didn't even seem upset that I had asked him; in fact, he thought it was a reasonable request.

MISTAKE #4: I let him write the IOU. I worried that he would be offended if I gave him one of my long, ugly, legal documents to sign. His one-sentence IOU was a bit muddy, specified the wrong amount, and did not say when he had to repay the money, other than "as soon as is practical."

As an attorney working on corporate deals, I always made sure the details were crystal clear. Why didn't I do the same in a transaction with my husband? Because I was afraid of insulting Mark. He would think I didn't believe him. A marriage is built on trust, right?

MISTAKE #5: I never asked to see his company's records. Nearly every dollar I had disappeared into his business account like dust sucked up into a vacuum cleaner. More than $40,000 in less than a year. I don't know what he spent it on.

I was just like those "surety wives," the subjects of research that culminated in the book *Sexually Transmitted Debt* by Belinda Fehlberg. She examined women who became liable for their spouses' business debts purely because of their intimate relationship, even if they derived no economic benefit from the transaction. She found that they did so because they had faith in their spouses, were preoccupied with their own jobs or with raising children, and were swayed by their husbands' complete confidence that their business ventures would succeed. See Chapter 3, *I Co-signed for You and Got Sexually Transmitted Debt*, for more on this topic.

By the time I loaned him my life savings, Mark no longer had a corporate credit card from his former job, and he claimed that he couldn't get one for his new business. So I made matters worse.

MISTAKE #6: I gave Mark a credit card for my own account.
I should have suspected he wasn't telling me everything about his financial situation, if he was unable to get his own credit card. I should have asked him questions. Lots of questions. Remember my Mistake #1: I didn't know anything about his credit history.

You're not surprised to learn that Mark charged thousands of dollars, are you? He turned out to be a "Credit Cad" who took advantage of my stellar financial record (see Chapter 3, *I Co-signed for You and Got Sexually Transmitted Debt*). It was so painful when I had to spend my entire Christmas bonus to pay his credit card charges.

To his credit (no pun intended), Mark did later cough up the $8,000 in credit card debt that he'd accumulated. He never returned the cash he'd borrowed.

When Mark launched his new architectural firm, he asked me to be on the board of directors, but I refused. This shred of common sense kept me from making yet another fatal mistake. Mark drove his company into bankruptcy; if I had been a director, I might have been held responsible. Wonderful.

When we married, I was vaguely aware that he'd had a previous small business, before we met. After I left him, I found out that venture had gone belly up too. I don't know the details of that chapter of his life, either. Never asked.

You can probably guess that Mark never forked out one dollar of the $52,000 he borrowed. He didn't even list me as one of his company's numerous creditors when he filed for bankruptcy.

I lost lots of cash and wound up with Empty Accountitis, but fortunately I wasn't stuck with his Sexually Transmitted Debt.

My ex-husband may have had good intentions to pay me back if his business succeeded.

However, there is no question that he was manipulative. He knew that I was the quintessentially supportive wife who would do anything to help him. He knew I would fall for the story that his cash flow problems were only a small bump in the rocky financial road of a new venture. He knew I had no clue that he had large debts and no more resources. He knew that I felt guilty asking him to sign an IOU. He knew that I trusted his repeated promises.

I was a naïve wife who made many critical mistakes. In the end, I was devastated, both financially and emotionally.

While I was angry at Mark, I was even angrier at myself for letting it all happen. I was also ashamed. Until I decided to write this book, only my family and a few close friends knew the story of what happened to me more than fifteen years ago, and why I got divorced.

I first "came out" about my experiences when I launched my blog, *Gold Diggers and Deadbeat Dads*, at *ValerieRind.com*. Buried in my profile, it said that I'd lost my life savings after I loaned money for a relative's startup business.

The folks at *The Huffington Post* spotted that one sentence and invited me to be a guest on a *HuffPost Live* segment on making loans to family members. It aired the day before Thanksgiving in 2013.

The Huffington Post then posted a short article, "My Ex-Husband Depleted My Life Savings," with excerpts from the video.

And out came the trolls!

If you're not a regular blog or online newsletter reader, you may not be familiar with this species. Trolls are people who post insulting or incendiary comments online, while hiding behind a pseudonym and faceless picture. Imagine someone sitting around with nothing better to do than criticize strangers by taking pot shots from the safety and anonymity of cyberspace.

The trolls made nearly three hundred comments about my story. The overwhelming majority said it was my fault I'd lost the money, that I had no one to blame but myself, and that I deserved what I got. They described me as stupid, dumb, a fool, a sucker, an imbecile, an idiot, a slow learner, a not very bright lady, a dumb broad, and — my personal favorite — "a sandwich or two short of a picnic."

The article was on the *HuffPo Divorce* page. It hit a raw nerve with lots of angry, spiteful, bitter people. You have to consider the demographic; I don't think most people surfing articles about divorce are looking for recipes or cute cat photos. Plenty of men grumbled that what happened to me was fair because women get alimony. I didn't quite understand the connection.

But dealing with the trolls (mostly by ignoring them) gave me the courage and commitment to talk about these issues even more publicly and in greater detail, and to help others feel less ashamed about their own situations.

Amira's story: From lender to loner

Amira and I met over coffee at a small local café. She told me how an initial $800 loan to her boyfriend Sean ballooned to more than $6,500 in less than nine months.

Gorgeous and articulate, Amira was in her mid-thirties. She had a Master's degree in biology, and was looking forward to getting her Ph.D. She had been involved with Sean for only a few months when he asked to borrow $800. Amira trusted him, so she didn't hesitate. He even signed an IOU.

Later he wanted another $500. She complied. Eventually, she asked him to pay back the $1,300 total. Sean promised that if Amira helped him pay a $1,500 debt he owed to someone else, he could get a $6,000 payday loan, which would enable him to give Amira the whole $2,800 he owed her.

This story sure sounded familiar to me. Just a short-term loan to a trusted loved one, right?

Amira went straight to her bank. "I told the teller, 'I can't believe I'm doing this.' I never took money out of my savings account, and certainly not as much as $1,500. It felt like I was stabbing myself in the stomach."

Amira and Sean had arranged to meet at a grimy payday loan place. Amira waited in vain for two long hours. Later, Sean had some lame excuse for why he hadn't shown up. Oh, they must have just missed each other, he said. Regardless, he hadn't been hired for the construction job he was counting on, so a payday loan was out of the equation.

As she sipped her latte, Amira admitted to me that all of this should have raised crimson flags, but she was an honest, trusting woman. No one had ever lied to her before. She liked Sean a lot, and she wasn't too upset about his $2,800 debt. They even joked about it. It was his idea to move in with her so she could "keep an eye on him."

Sean lied about working at non-existent construction jobs during the day and continued to manipulate and exploit Amira for money. He begged for another $600 so he could pay overdue child support for his three kids. Otherwise he would go to jail, he told her. Sean got angry when she first refused, and tried to make her feel guilty, saying, "You don't want me to go to jail, right? How can you say you care about me if you don't care about my kids?" Next, he claimed he needed $300 because his youngest son had landed in the emergency room without health insurance. Both times, Amira believed him because she thought, "No one would use his own kids to scam money out of someone."

Ker-ching — add another $900 to Sean's tab. His total was now $3,700.

One day, Sean had a minor car accident when he borrowed a friend's car. He called and told Amira the other driver said if they just paid her $300, she wouldn't report it to the police or the insurance companies. Sean put this woman on his cell phone to talk to Amira. The driver sounded a bit like she had been coached, but Amira sent the money to her by Western Union.

Sean now owed his girlfriend $4,000, and they had lived together for less than a month.

Things got even worse. Sean was arrested, sent to jail, and called Amira begging her to bail him out. Twice. He even tried to make her feel guilty for leaving him in jail until she could come up with the money.

Sean's outstanding loans at the Bank of Amira had now mushroomed to $6,500. She demanded that he pay her back. He promised, but he kept coming up with explanations for why he didn't have the cash.

Amira rationalized her tolerance of Sean. "I wanted to be a good person," she explained. "I'm a 'saver.' I thought that he only needed someone to care, be supportive, forgive him, and save his life."

The beginning of the end came the night Sean smacked her in the face. Amira called the police. The officers warned her to get rid of Sean, and they ordered him to leave the apartment. Sean soon found out that he had certain rights as a tenant even thought he'd never paid rent and he had no written lease. He even tried to get Amira evicted from her own apartment. Fortunately it didn't work.

A year later, he was still showing up at her door, pleading for forgiveness. He is out of luck. Amira got the financial disease I call Empty Accountitis. She has her eyes wide open now, and will never give Sean any more cash.

Amira never found out where all of her money went, although she says she suspects Sean was dealing drugs. But she's still dealing with the repercussions. Not only did she lose $6,500, she now works three jobs to pay off the thousands of dollars of credit card debt that piled up during that period in her life, while she supported Sean and drained her cash reserves. Her plans to get a Ph.D. are shelved indefinitely.

During her time with Sean, Amira went from being a lender to a loner. "I lost my friends and I ended up by myself," she told me. "I was embarrassed, especially when it got worse. I didn't want to look like a total screw-up."

She told a few close friends and her family and went to a therapist — the only person who she felt was not judgmental.

Amira learned to forgive herself. "People mess up. It's OK that I did. But it broke my spirit. It will take a lot for me to be able to trust again."

At the end of our chat, Amira said she felt that some good came out of this whole awful experience. She learned her biggest life lesson: She can depend on herself. Before, she'd always relied on a boyfriend to take care of her.

Amira was relieved when I explained I was writing this book about people who are exploited when they loan money.

For her, it meant that she wasn't "the only idiot on the planet." Far from it.

Vivian's story: Lies in exchange for loans

Vivian emailed me about her college roommate. Alice told Vivian a sob story about how Alice's mother had some medical expenses, because she had cancer. Alice needed to borrow $1,500 from Vivian for two weeks, until she got her student loan funds. Vivian didn't have a lot of spare cash, but she thought giving her roommate a short-term loan for such an important cause was the right thing to do.

But Alice never repaid the money, or paid any rent for their apartment. Vivian later found out that Alice's mother didn't even have cancer.

Alice also convinced her own mother to sell an investment that was set aside for tuition for the prestigious college that she and Vivian attended and for grad school. Instead of paying for her educational expenses, Alice used the money to get plastic surgery.

Alice's mother ended up filing for bankruptcy. We can safely assume this wasn't the first time that Alice had duped her mother.

Vivian ended her email to me, "Gee, now that I think about it, I should have given you Alice's mother's contact info so you could talk to *her* for your book."

Ken's story: "Because she's my sister"

A soft-spoken research analyst in his late fifties, Ken told me a story he has never told another soul. Ten years ago, he loaned more than $15,000 to his younger sister Katherine, so she and her husband Paul could buy a small vacation house in the mountains. Katherine's late mother-in-law had owned the house, but no one else in the family wanted to buy it. Katherine and Paul couldn't qualify for the mortgage (a definite "caution" sign Ken should have picked up on), so he decided to loan the money to his sister at a modest interest rate. Their agreement, which was never put in writing, was that Katherine would pay Ken back "when she could."

Katherine hasn't paid back any of the money. Not a penny.

Over the past decade, Ken has never asked his sister about the $15,000 loan. He didn't tell anyone else in their family. He knows Katherine has borrowed money from their parents, and that she hasn't repaid them either. Ken was the responsible one, and Katherine — well, for some reason the family always cut her a lot of slack.

You might think Ken would be angry or bitter about this loan to his sister, but he wasn't. At the time, he wasn't exactly thinking of it as a gift, but he calculated that it was an amount he could afford to lose. Ken told me, "The default was not a total surprise, but it was disappointing that she failed to pay back a debt. It's just not quite right."

I asked Ken why he agreed to loan the money to Katherine. He stared at me and quickly answered, "Because she's my sister. It was an opportunity for her to make a good investment. If I raised the issue, it would push us apart. My relationship with my sister is more important than money."

Ken's reaction may not be typical.

Alain's story: Collateral damage

A long time ago, Alain loaned $1,200 to a co-worker. Alain was smart enough to demand collateral in exchange for the loan, rather than accepting an IOU written on a scrap of paper. His co-worker left the company and never repaid the loan, so Alain kept the collateral.

Alain was now the owner of a pair of diamond stud earrings. He had no idea how much the jewelry was worth, but at the time of the loan he'd figured getting *something* would increase his chances that the guy would come up with the cash.

Years later — long after Alain had accepted that the $1,200 had vanished with the co-worker — he gave the diamond earrings to his wife. They were really tiny. You know, the kind that you have to squint at to see the stones. She was disappointed. Somehow the earrings had gotten bigger every time he told her the story. It seemed unlikely that they were worth anywhere close to $1,200.

Next time, get bigger collateral. Or don't loan the money.

What if someone asks me for a loan?

No one knows how many millions or even billions of dollars are loaned between friends and family members but never repaid. No requirement to formally report these transactions exists. Estimates of the default rate on interpersonal loans vary wildly. After all, how many people proudly announce at a cocktail party, "Hey, I got stiffed on a loan"? We are usually ashamed to admit our financial goofs. We don't want to look like a fool. I know I didn't.

So, when your cousin or sweetheart wants to borrow money, what should you do? I won't get all preachy and tell you that you should *never* be a lender. That's for you to decide. Every situation is different.

However, it's not necessarily an all-or-nothing proposition. You do have other options.

- You can loan a smaller amount.

- You can ask for collateral that you'll keep if the person skips out, like the diamond earrings that Alain got.

- You can agree to certain conditions. For instance, I spoke with a middle-aged investment banker, Elliott, who told me he was willing to lend $5,000 to his nephew Wayne to eliminate credit card debt, provided Wayne got regular budget counseling.

- You can suggest that the person borrow money online at an anonymous peer-to-peer site (sort of like eBay for personal loans) such as Prosper or Lending Club.

- Or you can just say no.

Please do learn from my seven mistakes. Let's recap:

MISTAKES #1 and #2: I was ignorant about my husband's financial past and present.

Do this instead: Ask lots of questions. Find out why your potential borrower needs the money. What will she spend it on? Medical expenses? Credit card debt? An investment that's supposedly too good to pass up? Ask why she doesn't have the cash. How else has she tried to get it? Why won't someone else help her? If she's starting a business, has she applied for a loan from the U.S. Small Business Administration? What about crowdfunding sites? How does she plan to pay you back? If she's knee-deep in debt and wants to borrow money to pay it off, then she is just trading one debt for another. What are the odds that you'll get your cash back if she handles her finances so poorly?

And I beg you, if the borrower is your fiancé or potential life partner, please read Chapter 6, *I Say 'I Do' to You, Your Assets, and Your Debts*, about commitment issues and the financial due diligence you should consider doing before taking a giant leap further into your relationship.

You also need to ask *yourself* some questions. Why are you considering this loan? Are you afraid of what the borrower will think of you, or of what he or she will do if you say no?

This is why money issues are so complicated when we mix them with our personal relationships. There's a whole lot more going on than just financial transactions.

MISTAKES #3 and #4: I didn't (initially) ask him for an IOU. The IOU was murky.

Do this instead: Although having a signed IOU from Sean didn't help Amira, a borrower may take the whole matter more seriously if your arrangement is formalized. Write the agreement yourself. It doesn't have to be a long, fancy contract. You can find a standard form of promissory note on the Internet. Let's just hope his "promise" doesn't make you "sorry."

While I'm generally not in favor of using legal documents that you download from Joe'sOnlineLawOffice.com, something formal is generally better than writing an IOU on the back of a booze-soaked cocktail napkin.

Both you and your borrower must sign and date the note. At a minimum, make sure it includes these details:

- Who is lending the money?

- Who is borrowing the money? It's critical to get this right if you are lending money to someone starting or running a business. Are you lending to the individual or to the company?

- How much is the principal amount?

- What is the interest rate? See below for more on why you should charge interest.

- What is the amount of each payment? There are plenty of online calculators to help you figure this out.

- When is each payment due? Perhaps you can time payments to coincide with your borrower's payday, or some other regular interval when they receive money.

- Will they give you collateral for the loan?

- What happens if the borrower pays late or misses a payment?

- When is the final payment date?

Consult a tax attorney or accountant, especially if the amount of the loan is more than $14,000. If you don't charge interest, the IRS may require you (not the borrower) to pay federal gift tax. This amount is based on the 2014 federal gift tax annual exclusion, but please get professional advice. You don't want to add insult to injury by creating a tax liability for yourself.

Consider using an online service such as ZimpleMoney that acts as an intermediary between you and your borrower to automate billing and payments. Having a bit of distance and formality may help you both treat the loan as more of a business transaction than an informal arrangement.

MISTAKE #5: I never asked to see his records.

Do this instead: After you hand over the cash, follow up with your borrower on a regular basis. How did he use the funds? Were his medical bills paid off, or did he purchase the latest electronic toys? If you loaned to invest in a business that was "a sure thing," keep a close eye on it. The success of that venture will determine whether you recover your money.

MISTAKE #6: I agreed to give Mark a credit card on my own account. This is a type of loan, although instead of lending cash, I let him "borrow" my credit. Your good credit is priceless, so don't give anyone the opportunity to trash it. You can read about joint and authorized users for credit card accounts, plus those scoundrels I call Credit Cads in Chapter 3, *I Co-signed for You and Got Sexually Transmitted Debt*.

Do this instead: Actually, I don't see any good alternatives here other than saying no.

Ouch! Now what?

Let's say you didn't listen to me, or you didn't find this book until it was already too late. You loaned money to someone and

Loans from YouBank

We started with traditional "brick and mortar" financial institutions, where you'd go to conduct all your everyday banking business with flesh-and-blood tellers. For significant transactions, such as mortgages, you met with the loan manager in his office. It was all personal and face-to-face.

Then came online banking. Now, you can open accounts, transfer funds, pay bills, deposit checks, and perform other types of ordinary transactions without ever talking to a real person. Most banks and other financial institutions have applications for your smartphone, so you can conduct nearly all of your banking business on the go.

Even as banking practices change, one thing remains the same: When you, an ordinary person, agree to loan money, it means you open a branch of YouBank. There are no FDIC protections for your personal finances. No rules or laws apply.

It's important that you understand that no matter what happens with your loan, you're changing the nature of your personal relationship with your borrower — forever. The balance of power shifts the moment you agree to bail out a friend or relative. The experience may bring you closer to each other. At the other end of the spectrum are true stories like mine and Amira's — those that ended in financial and emotional catastrophes.

At YouBank, the best approach is to always assume that you are giving a gift, not a loan that will be repaid. Never agree to lend an amount you can't afford to lose. Don't sacrifice your own emergency fund or retirement savings.

they didn't pay you back. What can you do to cure your Empty Accountitis?

Before resorting to strong-arm tactics, try this simple technique: **Ask the borrower for the money**. It could be that they genuinely forgot all about this debt and will be only too happy to make good on the loan. It does happen.

If you have a legal agreement with a deadbeat borrower, you can sue them if they don't pay. However, the right to sue isn't worth much, because you can sue anyone you want; winning is another story. Collection is a further challenge. Plus, filing a lawsuit means you have to invest your time and shell out money for court fees and expenses that you might not recover.

You can have your day in court, and you might triumph. The judge might bang his gavel and grant judgment in favor of the plaintiff (that's you). But if the borrower didn't pay you back because he's broke, your official court judgment isn't worth much. How is he going to repay you if he couldn't (or wouldn't) make good on the loan in the first place?

Winning a lawsuit may be an empty victory. If you get a judgment, you may need to look into options to collect the money, such as garnishing his wages. Unfortunately, this tactic assumes your borrower is gainfully employed and reports his income honestly — which may be unlikely for a person who wormed his way out of his obligations to you.

In the end, sometimes the best solution is to psychologically write off the loan. Let it go. If you try to force the issue too hard, you may damage your personal relationship with the borrower, possibly forever. He or she must have meant something to you in the first place, because most people do not lend large sums of money to casual acquaintances.

The best state of mind when loaning money to a friend or family member is: "I am giving a gift and I will never expect *anything* in return."

Conclusions

Next time — if there is a next time — you agree to be a YouBank lender:

- Think about the effect a loan might have on your relationship with the borrower.

- Formalize your loan agreement in writing.

- Assume you'll never be repaid.

- Don't lend money you can't afford to lose.

CHAPTER 3

I Co-signed for You and Got Sexually Transmitted Debt

In the late 1980s, a group called the Women's Credit Task Force, later known as WISER (Women Investigating Social and Economic Reform), became outraged at how the finance industry exploited women's economic power. The group, which consisted of Australian social workers, financial counselors, and lawyers, formed in February 1989 and later published a guide titled *How to Get Out of Sexually Transmitted Debt*. The guide was not intended to directly aid the victims themselves, but rather to educate lawyers and others to help their female clients.

Interest in the topic grew. Over one hundred people attended *Women and Credit: A Forum on Sexually Transmitted Debt*, in Melbourne, Australia on March 6, 1991. Speakers at this forum included financial managers, bankers, lawyers, financial counselors, consumer advocates, and government representatives. Apparently one of the presenters, Ms. Jenny Lawton, claims to have coined the term "Sexually Transmitted Debt." She quoted the text below, although she didn't provide the source:

> Once, women were unable to get loans in their own right. Times have changed, [sic] today they have improved financial status and discrimination in lending to women is illegal. But a new problem has been identified whereby women are being exploited for their improved financial status and are being duped into paying for the loans of others. I call this phenomenon Sexually Transmitted Debt.

The outcome of the forum was recommendations in four areas: specific legislative changes, self-regulation for lenders, programs for community education, and further research.

In the mid-1990s, judicial cases of women seeking to avoid liability for debts they had incurred related to their husbands' business ventures cropped up in courtrooms and became a topic of interest reflected in legal journals in the United Kingdom, Australia, and Canada. Belinda Fehlberg, now a professor of law at the University of Melbourne Law School, conducted an empirical socio-legal study in those jurisdictions about how a "surety" spouse provided loan security to a commercial lender and became responsible for his or her partner's debts. Fehlberg's work culminated in the publication of several law journal articles, and ultimately became the book *Sexually Transmitted Debt: Surety Experience and English*

Law in 1997, part of the series of Oxford Socio-Legal Studies that explores the role of law in society.

Fehlberg interviewed forty-nine British individuals between February 1993 and July 1994. The majority of these were sureties (mainly women) who became liable for their partner's loans. Other interviewees included a few debtor spouses, lenders, and lawyers.

The study results revealed that a woman often assumed that she should co-sign because helping her partner was a normal part of a marriage partnership. In some cases, a husband convinced his wife by coercion or even physical abuse. A wife might feel that she had no choice but to comply. These women rarely had any involvement in the running of their husbands' business ventures.

Fehlberg's ultimate finding was that there was a division between the "public" perceptions in the legal system — that the wives derived significant economic benefits from the transactions — and the "private" arrangements between intimate partners, where the surety spouses derived minimal financial advantages. Fehlberg concluded that legal reform was not necessarily the route to fixing the problem; instead, she recommended public education and further research.

The expression "Sexually Transmitted Debt" has become popular over the past twenty years in English-speaking countries including the U.S. It now refers to situations where a person in an intimate relationship becomes liable for his or her partner's financial obligations, such as credit card debt or co-signed personal loans, whether or not the person derives any financial gain from the arrangement.

Candace's story: "He said he would take care of everything"

I received a long email from Candace with anecdotes about several catastrophes, including classic examples of co-signing gone horribly wrong. She said she was duped by her boyfriend, Enrique, who told her he wanted to "pamper" her and "take care of everything financially."

Things were OK at the start, when they lived in her small apartment and split the rent. But then a court ordered Enrique to get a larger place, because he was divorced and needed separate rooms for his kids when they visited.

Candace and Enrique struck a deal: She would pay half the rent on their new apartment, and Enrique would take care of her monthly car loan payment.

It wasn't remotely close to an even trade. Half of the rent for the expensive townhouse to accommodate Enrique's kids far exceeded the amount of her loan payment.

When they split up, Enrique moved out. He promised to find someone to sublet so they wouldn't have to break their lease, but he never found a suitable tenant. So instead, Candace agreed to sublease the space to a "friend" who couldn't get her own apartment.

Yes, I'll bet you can see the handwriting on the apartment wall.

The friend moved in briefly but then disappeared — and of course she skipped out on paying any rent.

After that debacle, it became nearly impossible for Candace to sign a new lease elsewhere, even though she'd always paid her share of the rent for prior apartments.

And remember the other part of the deal — where Enrique was supposed to take care of Candace and "everything financially," including her car payments?

Well, of course he didn't. Enrique didn't make a *single* payment on the car. Candace didn't find out until much later, by which point she was so far behind she couldn't afford to catch up on the auto loan. Her car was repossessed.

Candace got "infected" with a nasty case of Sexually Transmitted Debt because of the apartment fiasco and the default on the car loan. While neither situation was technically her fault, her credit was decimated.

She told me other stories of emotional and economic hard times, and concluded:

> I try really hard not to look back. My love life and financial situation have been neck-and-neck terrible since Day One. When I was eighteen years old, my credit was *perfect*. I had a credit card right out of high school because my father gave both me and my sister credit cards to build our credit. The only stipulation was that we had to pay the *full* balance at the end of every month. I did that, and by the time I was twenty, my credit limit was somewhere around $20,000. I don't really remember, it was so long ago. But now my credit is ruined.

Sheila's story: "I'll put it on my account and you can pay me back"

You don't have to be in a relationship with someone to get saddled with his or her debt. Sheila contracted a non-intimate form of Sexually Transmitted Debt when she became ensnared in a co-worker's web of lies and debt. It started with $5 or $10 cash loans for lunch money and ended with her getting stuck with an expensive cell phone bill and astronomical charges for a rental car.

Sheila had her first supervisory position at a call center. She had a platonic relationship with one of her subordinates, a married man named Tim. Often he ran out of money a few days before payday and borrowed small amounts from Sheila, which he promptly repaid.

One day he asked to borrow $40, and she obliged. He paid her back with a starter check from his wife's account. Sheila realized in retrospect that this should have been an early warning sign. His next request was for $100; when his repayment check bounced, Tim gave her $125 to cover the loan plus the fee that her bank had charged for the bad check.

"This should have been another clue that something was not entirely kosher," she admitted to me while we chatted over coffee.

Friendship, just like love, can be blind.

Tim wanted a cell phone, and Sheila agreed that he could borrow hers. Then he wanted her to help him get his own phone. Always a smooth talker, Tim convinced the salesman to add his phone to Sheila's account. After only a month, Tim had far exceeded the data usage limit and had racked up a $600 bill. He promised to cut back his use, but he paid only $100 and stuck Sheila with the balance.

"I had to let the bill crash and burn because I couldn't afford to pay for the darn thing," she told me. "The concept simply didn't pass through his mind that *he* had to pay for it." Sheila's account became delinquent and it wrecked her credit history.

The next trick Tim pulled was to convince Sheila to get him a rental car for one week. He promised to pay her cash. Just before she received her credit card bill a few weeks later, the car rental office called her to authorize a monthly rental.

Sheila was shocked; she'd assumed Tim had returned the car on time.

The car rental manager was also bamboozled. Not only had Tim claimed that he'd paid Sheila for the car that he charged to her credit card, he'd also convinced the manager to let him rent *another* car. Tim paid cash for the second rental, but by the time Sheila got him to return the first car, the charges were more than $2,000. Tim never repaid her.

Eventually he was transferred and then left the company. Sheila believes that Tim was fired. He set up a meeting to repay her, but he didn't show up. Later she found out that Tim had frequently tried to borrow money from co-workers.

Sheila's judgment wasn't clouded by love or lust; how did her employee manage to take advantage of her so easily? Perhaps Sheila's desire to be nice and keep the peace at work blinded her to Tim's manipulative nature.

It began when she ignored the warning lights: small loans that became larger, the starter check, and then the bounced check. These were all hallmarks of a person who was irresponsible with his finances.

Adding Tim's cell phone to her account was the equivalent of co-signing for his charges. Renting a car for him gave him carte blanche to satisfy his transportation needs. Sheila's real downfall was that she didn't follow up to check whether Tim had returned the car. She got a non-intimate version of Sexually Transmitted Debt from this toxic financial relationship. Her credit score took a beating and it took a long time to improve.

Credit Cads

No, that's not a typo for "cards."

A "cad" is an old-fashioned term for a charismatic scoundrel who attracts ladies and then treats them dishonorably. Picture a tall man in a three-piece suit with a pocket square who acts like a gentleman with good intentions — only to disappear after a woman succumbs to his charms, leaving her devastated.

What I call a modern-day Credit Cad is a person (male or female) who takes advantage of your unsullied credit reputation.

You become a victim when you have a joint card account and the Credit Cad doesn't pay, or when you add an authorized user to your account who gets the benefit of your good standing only to leave you with piles of bills and a disgraced credit status.

This makes it perfectly clear, right?

U.S. federal law requires certain lenders to give a specific written warning to co-signers before they sign the contract, and the laws of other countries may require something similar:

- *You are being asked to guarantee this debt. Think carefully before you do. If the borrower does not pay the debt, you will have to. Be sure you can afford to pay if you have to, and that you want to accept this responsibility.*

- *You may have to pay up to the full amount of the debt if the borrower does not pay. You may also have to pay late fees or collection costs, which increase this amount.*

- *The creditor can collect this debt from you without first trying to collect from the borrower.* The creditor can use the same collection methods against you that can be used against the borrower, including suing you or garnishing your wages. If this debt is ever in default, that fact may become a part of your credit record.*

- *This notice is not the contract that makes you liable for the debt.*

*Depending on the laws in your state, this may not apply. If state law forbids a creditor from collecting from a co-signer without first trying to collect from the primary debtor, this sentence may be crossed out or omitted.

This warning explains what co-signing means in relatively plain and simple English. But most of us don't bother to read the fine print before rushing to click the "I accept" button.

Perhaps what it should say is:

• *Are you a complete idiot?*

When two people co-sign, they become equally responsible for the total debt in the eyes of the law, no matter what private agreement they have between them. If you are asked to co-sign a mortgage, loan, guarantee, or any other arrangement where someone else borrows money, it means only one thing: the bank does not trust them to repay. They want someone else — like you — on the hook as well.

Calculating the statistical risk that a potential borrower will duck his debts is part of the bank's everyday business. So before co-signing, ask yourself this critical question: If the bank experts crunched the numbers and don't believe your friend or family member will pay, why do you think you know better?

Do not co-sign unless you are confident that the borrower will live up to her obligations. She may have good intentions to repay the loan. However, co-signers often turn out to be fatally wrong about their assessment of the borrower's ability or willingness to pay.

Even if all goes smoothly and your friend or relative makes every payment on time, your status as a co-signer on that bank loan, rental, or other document can affect your own financial picture for years. Because the co-signed loan always counts as part of your own obligations, lenders may worry that you have too much debt. You may not be able to obtain a mortgage, personal loan, or credit when *you* need it.

Don't co-sign the loan if you can't pay it alone

People can be pressured into co-signing loans for lovers whose credit is less than stellar. Your partner may coax you by minimizing your obligation and saying, "It's not really your loan," "It's only a formality," or "Don't worry, you'll never have to pay."

However, the Federal Trade Commission offers a scary statistic: Almost 75 percent of co-signers have to pony up when certain loans go bad. These are not good odds for you as a co-signer. That statistic is from 1997, but it's doubtful that co-signers have fared any better in the twenty-first century.

Co-signing in relationships other than sexually intimate ones can also lead to problems. For example, a parent may agree to co-sign so her teenager can buy a tablet. The kid may not disappear, but it's still Mom's credit rating on the line if Junior's payments are late. And remember what happened to Sheila when

---

The "Singing" Co-signer

If you agree to co-sign, think of yourself as the diva's understudy. If anything happens to the star, the opera must go on. The audience doesn't want excuses. They paid a lot of money for tickets, they expect to see a complete show, and they certainly don't want a second-class performance.

If a primary borrower can't or won't pay her loan, you will be expected to step into her shoes without missing a beat. You are the Singing Co-signer.

If you agree to be a co-signer, break a leg.

---

she co-signed for Tim: His fiscal irresponsibility caused her credit score to plummet.

Not all co-signing is bad. For example, a parent might help his or her children get a head start on building credit, as it can be hard to get credit if you don't already have a credit history. But what about parents who take on legal liability for debts when their kids are older? Are they helping, or are they failing to teach their kids to be responsible for their own finances?

What if someone asks me to co-sign?

The first general rule: Don't sign anything you don't understand. Loan documents are ugly, but you must fully comprehend what your obligations are before you sign on the dotted line. Ask a lawyer or someone knowledgeable (but *not* the borrower, the bank, or their respective lawyers) to explain it to you.

You may have some leverage with the bank before you sign, because the deal is not going to happen without you or some other ~~sucker~~ co-signer.

Don't rely on verbal promises. All the details must be included in the written, signed contract. Keep a copy for your records. Make sure it says that the bank is required to notify you immediately if the borrower misses a payment.

Arrange for the lender to send you copies of all statements. You don't want to be blindsided.

Co-signing is perfectly acceptable in some situations. As discussed above, parents can help their kids learn responsible credit-building habits. When two people buy a house, the lender may require both names on the mortgage because each person has an ownership stake in the property. However, beware of co-signing for obligations where you get no tangible benefit.

Hurry up!

Never sign *any* legal document under pressure. In particular, be wary if the lender tries to rush or coerce you. The bank wants two people to sign even if there's nothing in it for you. Follow your gut instinct. Take your time until you're comfortable, even if it means delaying the loan. This may be difficult if the bank and your friend or relative are keen to close the deal right away. Just remember that you're signing up for a financial commitment that may last several years.

The lone (loan) alternative

There are other options to co-signing. If you have the funds available, you could loan all or part of the money (although please do read Chapter 2, *I Loaned Money to You*, about the dangers of lending to friends and relatives). Your risk, of course, is that they'll stiff you and it affects your personal relationship, but at least your credit score won't be decimated.

Joint user?

Many consumers are confused about arrangements in which two people have credit cards attached to the same account. There is a critical distinction between joint users and authorized users. Which one are you? It all depends on the fine print in your application.

If you both signed up and provided your Social Security number on the credit card application, you are most likely joint users. This is like being a co-signer. You're equally responsible for all charges racked up on the account even if the primary cardholder doesn't pay. The same applies if you're added to someone's existing account and you provide your Social Security number. Look for the words "joint and several," "liable," or "liability," especially where the credit card agreement refers to your obligations.

For better or for worse, you will share the entire credit history on this account, no matter who charged this or paid for that.

You're both rowing a tippy canoe. If the person you share the account with pays on time, it may improve your own credit. If, on the other hand, he or she pays late (or not at all), your credit score plunges. You might even get stuck with Sexually Transmitted Debt.

When things go south and joint users get divorced or otherwise go their separate ways, it's best if they can agree to do certain things so everyone can protect their credit history. First, close the account. Neither person will be able to add new charges — although, of course, you'll have to pay the existing outstanding amounts. Decide who is going to be responsible for which charges, and pay those promptly, or do balance transfers to your separate accounts.

You may be able to ask the credit card company to convert the joint account into two new individual accounts and transfer the balances as you direct. The credit card company may require you to reapply, and will consider your individual application based on your own credit history. You may or may not be able to get a new account with the same company.

CAUTION: Suppose you and your soon-to-be-ex-spouse agree to keep one of your joint credit card accounts open, and your divorce settlement includes specifics about who has to pay which bills or individual charges.

If your ex doesn't comply, the credit card company will still hold you both responsible. It sounds counterintuitive and unfair, but the fact that you've got a legally binding divorce decree doesn't matter to the credit card issuer. That document is between you, your former spouse and the court. The bank had no say in your divorce agreement, and therefore it doesn't care what it says. In the beady little eyes of the credit card company, you'll both always be liable for the debts, no matter what you agree privately.

Authorized user?

To help someone else establish or rebuild credit, a person with good credit can add the other person to his or her account as an authorized user. The authorized user gets a shiny credit card with his or her name embossed on it, but has no legal obligation to pay the bills. Practically anyone with a pulse can become an authorized user. Their own credit history (or lack thereof) is irrelevant.

You, as the cardholder, become the authorized user's friend with financial benefits, although you don't get anything tangible out of the deal. Read Chapter 2, *I Loaned Money to You*, to see what happened when I didn't hesitate to add my husband as an authorized user on my credit card account and he ran up the charges.

If your personal relationship with an authorized user goes sour, contact the credit card company immediately to revoke the user's privileges, and then close your account. Fortunately, it's not like co-signing for a deadbeat, where the bank won't let you out of the deal. It's your account and you're in charge.

Just think carefully about whom you add as an authorized user. There may be a good reason why certain people can't get their own cards.

What if the borrower doesn't pay up?

Sorry. If you've been duped into co-signing for someone who then skips out on their loan, your options are quite limited. You can try to get the bank to agree to remove a co-signer (you) from the loan, or to refinance the loan in the deadbeat's name alone, but most banks won't allow this solution. After all, they required a co-signer from the get-go. Both of you still owe the outstanding loan — plus you're now infected with Sexually Transmitted Debt and left with a wrecked credit profile.

At best, you could convince the lender or collection agency to settle the outstanding debt for less than the amount owed, in which case you'll pay it off either in a lump sum or in payments over a period of time. However, be aware that you may have to pay income tax to the IRS on the amount that was written off if the lender files a 1099-C form, which shows your "cancellation of debt" income. You don't get off the hook for free. Please consult with an accountant or tax attorney for professional advice.

CAUTION: Dealing with creditors and collection agencies is tricky and full of minefields. You don't want to inadvertently put yourself in a *worse* position. You can get detailed advice about bad debt and credit reporting from knowledgeable personal finance bloggers, as well as on websites like *myfico.com*.

But it's not all doom and gloom. Your reputation may not be sullied forever. A black mark on your credit report will have less significance as the years pass, provided you're zealous about paying all your bills on time.

Signing an apartment lease

If you sign a lease with anyone — lover, friend, acquaintance, stranger — it's the equivalent of co-signing a loan. Everyone whose signature is on that lease is responsible for paying the rent, regardless of how you divvy up the responsibility with your roommates. If a tenant doesn't pay his or her share, it's not the landlord's job to intervene. He wants the entire amount each month and can chase everyone to get it. If you have a history of unpaid rent, you might have a hard time getting a new place, because the landlord won't want to take a chance on you.

Be careful whom you move in with. Remember Candace? She learned this lesson the hard way when she and Enrique shacked up in an expensive apartment and then broke up.

Conclusions

Just like loaning money, co-signing can complicate your personal relationships. Sometimes we lose track of common sense practices.

To recap my suggestions about co-signing a loan or lease or adding a person to your credit card account:

- Always read the fine print.

- Don't sign any legal document you don't understand.

- Don't sign under pressure.

- Co-sign only if you are comfortable that the borrower will pay as promised.

- Consider lending money rather than being the "Singing" Co-signer.

- Beware of Credit Cads.

- Remember that a joint user of credit card accounts shares the payment obligations and the credit history, while an authorized user gets the benefit of the credit history but doesn't have to pay the bills.

- If you get stiffed by a co-borrower and wind up with Sexually Transmitted Debt, don't expect any mercy from the lender or landlord.

- Don't co-sign the lease or loan if you can't pay it alone.

- Assume that in the end, only you will be financially responsible.

CHAPTER 4

You're a Gold Digger

Wake up, guys: This isn't just a "women's" book

Here's the chapter for all you men who think there's nothing in this book for you because many of the victims are women.

The stereotypical gold digger is a young, greedy girl with expensive tastes she can't afford on her own dime. She often seeks to hook up with older, wealthy, balding men who drive convertibles.

Money-grubbing, manipulative wives or girlfriends can leave their unsuspecting guys broke or infected with Sexually Transmitted Debt.

People other than spouses or lovers can be gold diggers too. For instance, daughters can find ways to scam money from their dads.

Nicola told me about her mother and older sister:

> My father had a tough time taking care of two very demanding princesses who always needed designer clothes, furnishings, and cars. My father worked several jobs outside of his military career to support their addictions.

My sister claimed she got herself knocked up by a married officer, hoping to blackmail him. I don't even know if she was pregnant. She pulled this on a couple of guys and got one thrown in jail.

Jack's story: She took him for all he had

Jack was someone I knew quite well. He didn't tell me his story, but someone close to both of us did.

Jack was the victim of an exceptionally calculating gold digger. A successful orthopedist in Phoenix, he married Kristin many years after his first wife died of cancer. After being alone for so long, Jack was thrilled to have a new beginning with this charming woman.

But Kristin had her own plans. She knew she'd landed a great catch, a man who had worked hard his whole life to build a profitable medical practice, and she wanted a big chunk of it — quickly. At Kristin's insistence, the couple purchased an expensive new house and a sporty red BMW for her.

Just nine months after the wedding, Jack was astonished when Kristin filed for divorce. After less than a year of marriage, Kristin, who had contributed nothing, robbed Jack. And it was legal. Because Arizona is currently one of the nine community property states where the divorce courts split all marital assets evenly between the spouses, unless they have signed a prenuptial agreement, Kristin was entitled to half of the house, her car, and part of Jack's income earned during their marriage. Jack was also partially responsible for paying for the credit card debt that Kristin ran up during her frequent shopping trips and spa visits.

She manipulated him by establishing a relationship of trust and ensuring that they lived in the right place at the right time. Coincidence? I don't think so.

Worse, Kristin believed she was *entitled* to the cash and goodies because, as she herself put it, she had "no marketable skills." No one understood why Kristin's personal failure to be financially independent before she married Jack was a justification for grabbing the fruits of his labor after just a millisecond of matrimony.

Jack took a long time to recover from these financial and emotional disasters.

I was surprised to hear that he remarried — and moved to Nevada, another community property state. Jack passed away a few years ago, but I do know that he had a happy third marriage.

We consider many factors when deciding where we want to pitch our tent and call home. Before you say "I do," make a mental note that if you live in Arizona, California, Idaho, Louisiana, Nevada, New Mexico, Texas, Washington, or Wisconsin, you may be choosing to say "half will be yours" if you divorce (except for gifts and inheritances). Because the law varies in all states, it's wise to seek legal advice before you settle down or move. Please take a look at Chapter 6 about commitment issues (*I Say 'I Do' to You, Your Assets, and Your Debts*), such as whether to sign a prenuptial or postnuptial agreement.

Despite the stereotype of a scheming girl lusting after a rich man's money, women do not have the market cornered on this type of materialistic, unscrupulous behavior.

And yet, for all my ex-husband's financial foibles and faults, I don't consider him a gold digger. I think he truly loved me, and maybe even intended to repay the initial loan. However, he just kept digging himself deeper into debt, all the while telling me what I wanted to hear.

Gold Digger Seeks Sugar Daddy

The golden tides are turning sweeter. Modern lexicon is replacing the pejorative term "gold digger" with "sugar baby."

In some social circles, it's become more acceptable for a hot woman to openly search for a wealthy sugar daddy who will spoil and pamper her in return for no-strings-attached companionship.

Dating websites such as SeekingArrangement.com cater to people who seek these "mutually beneficial relationships."

The largest online enterprise in this niche is SugarDaddy ForMe.com, a site that claims to have four million members. You can search for a dizzying assortment of prospects: sugar daddies, sugar mamas, sugar babies (male or female), gay sugar daddies, and people seeking extra-marital liaisons.

In June 2014, the site's creator sponsored a free course called Sugar Daddy University. The seminar's objective was to explain "transactional relationships" and teach attendees how to hone their skills in the key areas of sexuality, understanding,

---

generosity, attraction, and reciprocity. Six hundred men and women participated.

It's a whole new, shiny world when "gold digger" is not a derogatory term and there's less stigma on bartering sex for money.

Or is it just plain old prostitution?

Hannah's story: "He threatened to kill me if I didn't give him money"

It was a pleasant afternoon in April — one of those first spring days when you can sit outside without feeling chilly — when Hannah and I shared iced tea on the porch of a local restaurant. An attractive woman in her late sixties, she told me about her three failed marriages. The details of the first two are not important to this gold digger story.

Her third husband, Frank, was a real lady-killer.

When we met, Hannah had recently retired from her job as a mid-level manager at a pharmaceutical company. Her story starts fifteen years earlier, when her only daughter was grown and Hannah moved across the country to Seattle. You may know someone like her who made a gutsy life change and relocated — alone — to a new place where no job, family, or friends were waiting when she arrived.

Hannah dated using online services like Match.com and eHarmony. She stumbled upon Frank, who was eight years her junior.

It wasn't a romantic connection at first; they were platonic friends for about a year. Instead, he acted as her local guide because he had lived in the Seattle area his whole life.

"Frank played it well," Hannah told me. "He showed me the city and local neighborhoods, but he maintained the boundaries of our friendship."

A natural-born salesman, Frank could hawk anything. When they met, he was peddling mattresses. He was good at it. Of course, Hannah didn't realize it at the time, but that is one of the hallmarks of a skilled con artist: being able to reel people in without them realizing it.

Watercolor painting was Hannah's hobby. By coincidence (or so it seemed), Frank said he'd always wanted to be an artist. He asked her to teach him the advanced skills. On the weekends at her apartment, they worked on large canvases together.

Hannah achieved some modest success with her artwork. Frank wasn't jealous; instead, he was her biggest supporter. He volunteered to act as her marketing coordinator, using her money to promote her efforts when she presented her paintings at local exhibitions.

Later, she realized that Frank had no genuine interest in painting, or even in art. "That's what pulled us together," she explained to me several times. "He told me I was helping him fulfill his lifelong dream."

After they'd been involved for a few months, Frank invited Hannah to spend a weekend away at a local winery. It wasn't an extravagant trip, and he took care of all their expenses. However, on the drive back to Seattle, he asked her to pay half. She wasn't willing; her position was that he invited her, so he should pick up the whole tab.

"I suppose I should have seen this early indication that he was keeping track and I was expected to split everything," she said. "How people handle their finances is a good indicator of the condition of your relationship. His behavior was a sign of his not being straight with me about money."

One day, out of the blue, Frank asked her, "What are your retirement plans?" She thought it was a casual question, and revealed that she had inherited an expensive house in Key West. She received a steady stream of rental income and planned to sell it when she retired.

We all have perfect views of our world in hindsight.

At the time, Hannah didn't realize the significance of what Frank asked. He wasn't merely curious about how she envisioned her golden years. He was formulating his own plan. One that would culminate in his claim to half of that grand Florida property.

Their relationship progressed. She encouraged him to get better sales jobs and he increased his salary substantially. Because Frank grew up as the under-achiever in a family of stars, he felt good that he had achieved financial success. Hannah and Frank now earned about the same amount of money.

Hannah decided to give marriage a third chance when she wed Frank, and they bought a house in a quiet Seattle suburb. Frank took $25,000 out of his retirement funds for the down payment. The house needed substantial remodeling, so Hannah borrowed $350,000 against the Key West property to pay for the work.

As an aside — they didn't realize that this fiscal plan was flawed. It was a bad move for Frank to decimate his 401(k) account and pay penalties for an early withdrawal, and for Hannah to take a home equity loan on a rental property. But this was only the start of the couple's poor financial choices.

Frank and Hannah signed a written agreement that he would pay half of the monthly loan repayments on the $350,000 Hannah had borrowed to fix up their house. He held up his end of this bargain for only one year.

"It was painful to get the money from him each month," Hannah told me. "We had separate bank accounts, as well as one joint account for our shared expenses. I paid most of our bills, because Frank had a daughter from his first marriage to support. But he always seemed to have money to pay for his own fun things while I was stuck paying for the ordinary household expenses."

Hannah insisted that they take care of their estate planning. She put Frank's name on the title of the Key West property, as trustee for her daughter. This meant that Frank didn't own and wouldn't inherit the house if Hannah died. His legal obligation would be to ensure that her daughter got the property. It was a critical distinction. Frank pretended that he didn't really understand the arrangement. But he was a lot smarter than he appeared to be.

Their marriage started to fizzle after about three years. "He got tired of me as his wife," Hannah sighed. "He told me that he had a right to get his sexual needs met elsewhere. He had always been flirtatious."

I asked her if Frank was good-looking. "No," she said emphatically. "He was ugly. But he had a way with women. He was persuasive, complimentary, and the women were drawn to him. My friends just adored him."

They tried marriage counseling. She couldn't see it at the time, but Frank expertly manipulated both her and their trained counselor. They were given assignments and made agreements, but Frank never complied.

Frank's extra-marital flirtations became more obvious, and she found out he was having a physical affair. She printed out the emails she found on his computer in case she needed them later for evidence.

Divorce was the obvious next step for the couple. Frank first proposed the terms. He thought Hannah should give him $100,000. He offered no calculations to support this amount. It sounded like he'd just pulled a number from the sky.

In the kitchen after dinner one night, he casually told her, "You're a diabetic, so I could give you a fatal overdose of insulin. It would look like you made a mistake. No one would ever know. I'd get away with it. The Key West house and everything else would be mine. So you might as well give me what I want now."

When I heard this part of Hannah's story, I suddenly felt very chilly. I wanted to drink something stronger than iced tea.

Hannah was in shock and couldn't sleep for a week. One afternoon when she was out with friends (whom she still hadn't told about Frank's death threat), she fainted. The doctors concluded her ailment was stress-related; she didn't tell them about her recent colossal trauma.

Frank rushed to the hospital. He fooled everyone, playing the part of the loving, caring husband. He also tried to convince Hannah to sign a document to give him control of the trust if they divorced. She was foggy from the medication but still alert enough to know to stand up to this gold digger and not sign any papers he shoved under her nose.

She tried to press charges against Frank, but there was no evidence without witnesses to his extraordinary threat.

Their conflicts continued and turned violent. According to Hannah, he lied to the police and said she threatened him with a letter opener. She claimed that she was slitting open sealed letters, and she pointed at him mid-sentence for emphasis. It looked like a typical domestic violence case of he-said-she-said. The police told Frank to leave, because standard practice was to get the man out of the house.

Frank broke into the house when he knew Hannah was away on vacation. He stole evidence about the Florida property and the emails to his girlfriends.

To reduce her housing expenses, Hannah got a female roommate. Frank climbed in through a window to scare the roommate and had her served with an eviction notice because his name was still on the title of the house. Hannah and her roommate went to Small Claims Court. The judge knew Hannah and Frank because they already had a long history of trying to get restraining orders against each other. He had heard enough and threw them all out of the courtroom.

The divorce process wasn't pretty, of course. Frank hired a shark in a suit who claimed that Frank owned half of the Key West mansion. Remember, his name was indeed on the title, but as a trustee for Hannah's daughter. Frank had no legal claim to the property as an actual owner himself. Hannah and her family had owned the property for thirty-five years before she married Frank. He had contributed nothing.

After two years and $100,000 in legal fees for arbitration, she got to keep her own house.

I asked Hannah how Frank got a female lawyer to take his case when it seemed obvious (to me, anyway) that he had no legal right to the house. She thought that it was yet another instance of how Frank could pull people — particularly women — into his story, and that he must have portrayed his situation to the lawyer as, "Poor me, this woman [Hannah] is trying to take everything I own."

During the divorce, Frank filed for bankruptcy. That meant he had no further obligations to pay for the home remodeling loan.

Looking back, Hannah realizes that she was vulnerable when she met Frank. He saw her weakness, just like a bird that spots a wounded worm in the ground.

"He said and did all the right things during the early stages. I trusted him," she said.

Hannah noted a common tactic among conniving men who sing the song of "Please help me to be a better person!" They know it will appeal to a woman's motherly nature to help people — particularly men who appear to be insecure.

She theorized that a woman's emotional reaction is, "Here's someone who will appreciate what I do." In her case, Frank pretended to respect her artistic talent and aspire to cultivate it in himself.

According to Hannah, gentlemen of a certain age (over sixty-five, she estimated) talk quite openly among themselves as "looking for a nurse or a purse" to take care of them. Men, who in their prime years were stalked by money-hungry girls, can become gold diggers in their sunset years.

Hannah's not going to meet the financial, physical, emotional, or other needs of another weak man. She put the Key West property on the market and will spend the proceeds enjoying her retirement. Hannah owns the house that she and Frank bought and shares her expenses with a roommate. Having the companionship of another divorced woman in her sixties is a bonus.

Yet she admitted she dates new men on occasion. I was surprised to hear that she hadn't ruled out a fourth marriage.

Of course, I still couldn't forget that Frank had threatened her in a cruel and cold-hearted attempt to score a better divorce settlement.

"Do you think he would have gone through with it?" I asked her.

Hannah paused and said yes, she thought Frank might have tried to kill her.

We'll never know.

Hannah heard that Frank hoodwinked and married another woman.

She died. Circumstances unknown.

Denise's story: "My boyfriend was a mooch"

Denise emailed me a succinct version of her story:

> Basics: Newly divorced; i.e., stupid. Let some mooch (uh, in that day I called him a boyfriend) talk me into signing an apartment lease, buying a $22K car which I couldn't afford, paying all the bills, putting the utility bills in my name while fronting the deposits, buying a motorcycle for him to drive which I also could not afford, contributing to his drug habit, getting personal loans, and eventually filing bankruptcy on $65K of debt before it was all said and done.
>
> To say I was stupid is the understatement of the year. How did this happen, you ask? He was an EXCELLENT salesman and I bought every single damn word he said. I was stupid, plain and simple, bought the t-shirt, grew from it.

Denise didn't specify what the guy was "selling" in order to trick her into buying.

How to time your divorce for the best result

I heard this story third-hand, but it sounds plausible. After about nine years of marriage, a woman decided she wanted a divorce.

But she didn't say anything to her husband, because she knew that she'd be eligible to receive part of his retirement or Social Security benefits only if they were married for at least a decade. She hung in there until just after their tenth anniversary celebration and then summoned her divorce lawyer. Now that's some genuine gold digging behavior, a decade after she'd tied the knot.

Quiz: Are you a gold digger?

There's a short informal quiz titled "Are You a Gold Diggin' Woman?" offered by *Blogthings.com*. It has eight what-would-you-do multiple-choice questions to test your opportunistic tendencies (see Resources section for the link).

For example:

A guy you've been dating for only two weeks gives you an expensive bracelet at dinner. You:

> *(a) Thank him for the gift — and give him something nice the next time you go out*
>
> *(b) Make a big deal about it, say he spent too much, but end up keeping the gift (and feeling a bit uncomfortable about it)*
>
> *(c) Smile and accept. Score!*

If you pick all the "(c)" answers, you're pegged as a genuine gold digger. However, according to the experts at Blogthings, that's *not* a negative quality. It's OK to be superficial. You're

---

entitled to be "rewarded" for all your hard work to look attractive, but it's a deal breaker if a guy doesn't have a big enough wad of cash.

I have a hard time understanding why anyone would be proud to be categorized as a gold digger.

There are no wrong answers. On the other side of the gold doubloon, if you pick all the "independent woman" answers, the quiz creators see it as a positive thing — you've got plenty of your own cash and you're not interested in being some older dude's trophy girlfriend.

The middle of the road is a Silver Digger. For these women, income isn't the sole factor when they decide whether to date a guy, but they'll never turn down a free meal.

All that glitters

Beware. It's easy to be swept away by someone who fakes romantic interest to secure a better lifestyle with you.

How do you spot a lover with ulterior financial motives?

A "May-December" romance is not an automatic indicator that the younger person has dollar signs in her eyes rather than true love in her heart.

My husband, Mark, was significantly older, and by all outward appearances, he was successful. I know that some people viewed me as a freeloader. The irony was that I lost all my own cash when his startup business flamed out.

Ask yourself whether your new love interest seems overly curious about your financial situation. Wanting to know too much too soon might be a bad sign. Remember Frank, who asked about Hannah's retirement plans so he could scheme a way to make his *own* future more cushy — but without her in the picture.

However, just because someone is inquisitive about your economic health doesn't mean they want to take advantage of you. In fact, it's critical to understand each other's financial status if your relationship is progressing into the serious zone — see Chapter 6, *I Say 'I Do' to You, Your Assets, and Your Debts.*

It's not only about where a person rates you on their scale of wealth. Look at how they handle their *own* finances. We all make mistakes and struggle from time to time (or longer). But it's a warning sign if your friend or loved one continues to make poor decisions, such as buying shiny luxury items instead of paying the household bills. You don't want to become their Bailout Billy.

Conclusions

If you are getting involved with someone of lesser means, take it slowly. Try not to let lust overcome your common sense. Give the relationship time to develop. Avoid making major financial moves too quickly, such as changing your will to leave a significant amount of money to your new lover, or adding them to your credit card accounts.

Unfortunately, there is no guarantee you won't be swindled by a shrewd opportunist who excavates your gold and runs.

CHAPTER 5

You Also Physically Abused Me

This chapter is about people who commit the hideous combination of financial abuse and domestic violence. Their partners may become tragic victims of "coerced debt," a newly recognized phenomenon.

Tina's story: She took the rap for him

"Love is totally blind," sighed Tina, a petite woman now in her early twenties who stayed with a violent boyfriend for years. They started dating when she was sixteen, and she continued to "allow him to take advantage of me," she told me on the phone.

Tina gave Leroy money and did whatever he wanted to keep him "happy." She complied because she feared he would leave her.

One night, Leroy beat her up so badly that the police arrived and wanted to arrest him. All Tina wanted was for Leroy to stop beating her and threatening her with guns and knives. For unknown reasons, even though Tina was obviously battered, the officers didn't take photographs of her bruised and swollen face.

While Leroy languished in jail, he reminded Tina that his mother had recently had a heart attack. If Tina had him arrested, it would be too much for his poor mother to handle, he said. Leroy's mom would surely have another heart attack and die. He snarled, was *that* what she wanted to happen?

No one seemed too concerned about Tina and her injuries. Strangely, Tina's own mother sided with Leroy. So Tina and her mother cooked up a plan to get Leroy out of jail and save his mother from her certain imminent death: Tina would tell the police that she made the whole thing up.

But that wasn't the end. Tina was fined $2,000 for filing a false police report. Her driver's license was suspended. Getting a job became difficult because she had a criminal record.

Tina told me that shortly after Leroy got out of jail, she bought him an MP3 player for what she called an "I'm sorry" gift. I don't know what she was apologizing for.

Tina took the rap for Leroy's physical abuse and financial manipulation. All for love.

When we spoke, Tina had already left Leroy and was in another relationship. I hope it was a healthier one.

Wendy's story: "He did it for the drug money"

Wendy married when she was young and naïve, before she knew that Peter was a violent meth addict.

Her descriptions of physical abuse horrified me.

Wendy wrote about "car crashes that ended up with me in a ditch, being thrown through a sliding glass door, etc."

I couldn't even imagine what "etc." included.

After six months of severe domestic violence, she gathered her strength, filed for divorce, and moved to another town sixty miles away. Wendy had a wonderful chance for a new beginning, free from abusive Peter.

But her troubles weren't over.

One morning she stepped outside to go to work, and her car was gone. Wendy called the police, who found out that the bank in her old town had repossessed it. She didn't understand; she'd paid cash for the car a few years earlier. How could it be repossessed if she'd never had an auto loan?

Finally she figured it out.

Desperate for drug money, her ex-husband Peter had gone to that local bank to get a personal loan. He'd put up Wendy's car as collateral after he found that she'd left the car title in a drawer in her rush to pack.

The loan officer was evidently missing a few dollars out of his mental cash drawer. He'd let Peter bring the papers to Wendy to sign at her office. Wendy, of course, wasn't a part of this plan; Peter had forged her signature. He got the loan — and before long, skipped out on the payments. Then the bank seized Wendy's car.

It took a lot of time and legwork for Wendy to get her car back. It took even longer to get rid of her Sexually Transmitted Debt. The car repossession stayed on her credit report for years, a blotch like a black eye that she'd suffered by his hands.

LaShanda's story: "It's the price I had to pay to get rid of him"

LaShanda was a shy secretary in her mid-thirties who met me for coffee on a brisk day in October.

Neither of her ex-husbands "knew how to treat people," she said.

LaShanda told me that her first husband became a deadbeat dad who failed to support their two young kids. She didn't do any better when she married Leon, who subjected her to constant physical and verbal abuse.

Leon was manipulative and controlling. LaShanda was required to call him "to check in" whenever she wasn't at home.

Oddly, Leon didn't want them to have a joint bank account. He preferred to have separate accounts, so that he could demand money from her. He also forged checks on her personal account.

LaShanda bravely went to the District Attorney's office, but they weren't willing to prosecute Leon because not enough money was involved. Each of the forged checks was under $250, below the legal limit for a felony charge.

Leon was obsessed with buying and selling sports memorabilia on eBay and Craigslist. He made some money from these trades, but he always used it to buy more stuff.

LaShanda received $75,000 from a worker's compensation settlement, but Leon snatched it and spent it online instead of paying her medical bills.

She bought a car; he made her sell it back to the dealer for half of what she'd paid because Leon wanted cash.

The electricity in their house was turned off. Later, he declared bankruptcy.

She always knew that Leon was immature. "I was raising three kids — his and mine — and I guess I had four because I took care of him too. He was totally irresponsible. You'd think a fifty-year-old man would know how to act. But he thought if you didn't *want* to pay bills, you didn't have to."

When LaShanda fled, she had no car or other possessions, and had to stay with a friend. Leon fibbed and told everyone that he'd thrown her out.

While she lost a lot of money during their disastrous marriage, LaShanda philosophically said to me, "It's the price I had to pay to get rid of him."

Now living with her daughter, who is in her mid-twenties, LaShanda looked on the bright side. "Every day, it gets better ... I've come a long way and I'm only going to get better."

Coerced debt

Each of the three women featured in this chapter suffered at the hands of a dangerous, exploitative man.

Wendy and LaShanda were victims who experienced a phenomenon called "coerced debt." This phrased was coined by Angela Littman, an assistant professor at the University of Texas School of Law who performed the first comprehensive research and analysis of "financial abuse perpetrated through consumer credit."

It is a complicated dynamic. Littman explains that abusers coerce, deceive, and manipulate their victims into debt.

For example, an abuser may obtain credit cards in the victim's name without her knowledge or consent, force her to take out loans for his benefit, or trick her into signing over the deed to the family house.

Wendy's anecdote is a vivid example of a coerced debt situation. Her violent husband Peter surreptitiously put her car up as collateral for his loan, failed to pay, and left her with a terrible credit history. LaShanda's second husband Leon forced her to open a separate account so he could write bad checks.

Littman says that the problem of coerced debt is complex because there is another player that is inextricably involved, along with the abuser and the victim: the commercial lender.

It's similar to the housing financing crisis that happened a few years ago, in terms of how difficult it can be to place blame. Fingers point at the three possible culprits — the abusive husband, the uneducated wife, and the lender who extends credit without asking enough questions.

Who's to blame in these murky situations?

Did the husband deceive or coerce his wife — or did she freely agree to the transaction?

Because of increased demand for consumer credit, banks and financial institutions have modernized and automated their application systems, making access to credit and loans easier. You can apply online and get approved for a new credit card in less than a minute.

Should the lender in questionable transactions probe deeper? What can lenders do if live human beings aren't running the approval systems?

Conclusions

It's incredibly difficult for a victim to extricate himself or herself from a toxic relationship that involves both domestic violence and financial exploitation, especially if he or she has been coerced into Sexually Transmitted Debt. Maybe a young woman doesn't have her own money to leave. Even if she does, her bad financial track record may prevent her from getting housing, access to credit, and even employment. It's a vicious cycle.

Coerced debt is yet another type of economic problem that intimate couples face, and we need to understand it better in order to prevent its devastating consequences.

CHAPTER 6

I Say 'I Do' to You, Your Assets, and Your Debts

P lease read Chapter 1, *You Lied to Me*, which shares my unfortunate story and shows why you must know the economic history of your future partner before you marry or get seriously involved.

Do not stick your ostrich head in the financial sand because you're afraid of what your partner will think if you ask such personal questions.

If you're already committed, it's never too late to have a financial open house.

Hal's story: He saw the light when the electrician showed up

"You think you know someone well, that you love and want to marry them, but you don't *really* know them until you live with them," Hal grumbled to me over a few beers. He is a forty-something graphic designer who almost made a fatal financial error by marrying Fiona, an underemployed writer.

"Fiona sheepishly told me just before we got engaged that she had accumulated about $15,000 in credit card debt," said Hal. "I told her it wasn't a deal killer and we'd come up with a plan for her to pay it off. We started living together, but after a few months I noticed she wasn't opening all of her bills. Finally, I confronted Fiona. I said I needed to know how much debt she really had."

Fiona's situation was not unusual. Simply put, she liked fancy restaurants and skiing vacations, but she didn't have the income to support her desired lifestyle.

Her way of dealing with debt? Denial. For months, she'd discarded, misplaced, or refused to open her bills. So Fiona had no idea how much she owed; the $15,000 figure was a guesstimate. She had never even seen her credit report.

After Hal insisted that she get a copy of her report, Fiona was shocked to learn that she was now $40,000 in the red — and that one credit card company had already sued her.

Hal wasn't too surprised, because he knew that by ignoring the bills, Fiona's debt problem was growing exponentially worse. He wasn't pleased about it, but he still thought they could overcome this problem together.

(Note: This story took place in ancient times, when people shared landline phones and answering machines at home.)

The collection agencies wasted little time finding Fiona after she moved into Hal's house. At first, they sounded like telemarketers, because they left messages to call "Mr. Jones" at a toll-free number. They made it sound important, but gave no indication of the reason for the call. Hal was annoyed that his phone rang all the time. The voicemail was full of insistent messages. Fiona found these calls stressful, and she refused to answer the phone unless she knew the caller. Her stress-related health conditions, including anxiety attacks and migraines, grew steadily worse.

While downing another beer with me, Hal went on to say that early one morning, someone pounded on his front door. He and Fiona were in bed, but they were too afraid to answer it. The couple assumed that a sheriff had arrived to serve Fiona with a summons. Fiona cowered under the covers. Hal peeked through the curtain, holding his body stiffly back from the third-floor window, hoping that the sheriff wouldn't see that someone was at home.

It turned out to be the electrician, who was scheduled to do some repairs. Hal had forgotten all about the early morning appointment. "I had never been so happy to see him," he laughed wearily.

Hal saw the light in that one instant. Things had gotten way out of control when he became a prisoner in his own home. This was not the life he'd envisioned with Fiona.

Not long after, he broke off their engagement. It was heartbreaking for him, but better to find out the truth before Fiona became his lawfully wedded wife and drowned them both in debt.

The debt itself wasn't the problem for Hal; it was Fiona's way of dealing with it. Or, more accurately, *not* dealing with it. He summed up, "In the end, I decided I couldn't marry someone who was so irresponsible with her finances, even though I loved her."

Because the premarital debt was all in Fiona's name, it may not have become Sexually Transmitted Debt for Hal if they got married. However, it would have directly affected their lives. Even if she changed her ways, Fiona's meager income would have been gobbled up to pay down her debt for many years, rather than contributing to a solid financial lifetime with Hal.

Monique's story: "I was so into our future together"

Monique and I met for coffee, and she told me about the cash she lost because of her ex-fiancé Felipe. She was in her mid-thirties and described herself as "too young to be a sugar mommy."

Monique paid for Felipe, who was unemployed, to attend a seminar about starting a small business. He prepared a basic business plan for an overseas agricultural venture, but she thought it required too much initial investment, particularly because he didn't have much in the way of savings. Felipe didn't revise the plan and instead convinced Monique to invest in his business.

"He said it would be 'our future' and I'd never have to work again," she told me. "Felipe would run the company and I'd get to live like a queen."

This picture appealed to Monique, so she plunked down more than $10,000. Felipe moved overseas where the business was located, so Monique had no visibility into the operation. Felipe claimed he spent a lot of the initial capital that she fronted on construction expenses.

Monique was dubious. "I'd like to believe there's a building somewhere, but to be honest I'm not even sure," she told me. "I was just *so* into our future together."

Monique described herself as someone who was normally frugal and wise with her money. She acknowledged that it was unusual for her to not only contribute to fund this dicey startup venture, but also to send money for Felipe's clothing and daily expenses. Monique even paid for his mother's funeral costs.

Everyone told her that Felipe was using her, but she was utterly in love. "I gave to him with my eyes closed. I focused on building our future together," she explained to me. "I considered us like a married couple already. The only thing missing was a church wedding."

She broke up with Felipe as soon as she found out he was cheating on her.

Monique ended up as a victim of sexual and, most likely, financial infidelity. "I didn't pay attention," she admitted. "I put my whole trust in him. I never thought that anything like this would happen."

Strip down to the details

Before you marry, shack up, commingle your money, or buy a house together, I think it's critical that both partners share the details of their financial pasts, particularly if either one — or both — has a pattern of poor economic management.

Make a detailed inventory of your assets and debts — warts and all. It may signal future problems if you don't trust the other person enough to tell him or her about your student loan debt, your bulging bank account in the Cayman Islands, or your upcoming IRS audit. You each need to know exactly what you're getting into. You don't want to be blindsided later.

What's the score?

According to a 2011 poll by Harris Interactive® on behalf of the National Endowment for Financial Education, 57 percent of the adults who married in the past five years or who planned to get married in the next year knew the credit score of their partner before marriage, while 43 percent did not. It's encouraging that a majority had shared this information. I wish more engaged couples paid closer attention to this detail than to the seating plan for their wedding reception.

It's a good idea to share your recent credit reports with each other, because you can't hide anything there. Get a free copy of your three credit reports every year at *annualcreditreport.com*. If you don't understand the reports, go to a comprehensive website like *myfico.com* for detailed information. Or find a reputable credit counselor who can provide objective advice, perhaps through the National Foundation for Credit Counseling or the Association of Independent Consumer Credit Counseling Agencies.

If your partner has substantial debt that he accumulated before the wedding day, it's possible (although not guaranteed) that you may not get Sexually Transmitted Debt if the accounts remain in his name. However, as Hal realized, that debt may live with the two of you for years. You'll need a big, red line item in the household budget for credit card or student loan payments.

Do you plan to buy a house? Lenders will calculate the total amount of household debt. Did you know that they tend to rely on the middle of the three credit scores when determining the interest rate and other terms of your mortgage?

Now for the difficult questions

I'd rather not be ten years into another marriage before I know the score — and I mean more than the credit score.

Here are questions that I suggest you and your partner ask each other, if you haven't already. You certainly won't be able to tackle them all in one evening, but you can work through the issues together in stages.

The moral of the story: Kiss and tell.

•   Have you ever been married?

People may conveniently leave out a little detail like a brief failed marriage when they were young. They may reduce the number of times they have been wed because they worry that they won't be attractive to you if they have too many ex-spouses. As discussed in Chapter 1, *You Lied to Me*, people often distort the truth to look better if they are insecure about themselves and worry about how they think others may judge them.

•   Are you currently married? Separated? Legally divorced?

It sounds crazy, but there are true stories of people who manage to live a double life where neither family is aware of the other's existence. Countless individuals cruise online dating websites claiming to be available when they're actually married, saying they're separated while still living with their spouse, or swearing they are "*seriously* planning to leave my wife soon."

- Do you pay or receive alimony? When will that obligation end?

- Do you have any kids? Are you required to pay child support? Do you pay it?

If a potential spouse has to support existing children, it could have a dramatic effect on your financial future for many years, or even decades. You don't want to get involved with a certified deadbeat parent, especially if you plan to have children together.

- Do you want to have (more) children?

This is a critical issue on many fronts, because the number of kids you raise is a major factor in your economic picture. Discuss your financial approach to childrearing — everything from your views on cash allowances to whether saving money for college education is a top priority.

- Do you have any addictions to alcohol, drugs, or gambling?

Be aware that people with these problems may not tell you the whole truth.

- Have you ever been arrested? Convicted? Are you on probation?

- How much do you earn?

- How much money do you have in cash? Stocks? Mutual funds? Gold bullion?

- What are the deductions from your paycheck?

- What is your net income?

- What percentage of your income do you save?

- How much do you have in an IRA, 401(k), or other retirement accounts?

- When do you plan to retire? What's your plan to get there?

- Do you budget your money? How?

- Do you spend more or less than you earn each month?

- Do you donate to charities? How much? Which causes or organizations?

- Do you have a will and trust? Powers of attorney? Advance directive?

- Do you have short-term and/or long-term disability insurance? Long-term care insurance? Life insurance? How much? Who is the beneficiary?

Read the stories in Chapter 8, *Where There's a Will, There's a Relative*, about what can happen if you never sign a will or if your estate documents are outdated.

- Has anyone sued you? What's the worst-case scenario if you lose, including the costs of your lawyer's fees?

- Do you own a business?

Examine the company's financial records for the past three years. Get an accountant to review these documents if you don't understand them. If the company doesn't keep adequate financial records, you should be very worried.

Please read Chapter 2, *I Loaned Money to You*, about my failure to ask the right questions about my husband's venture. You can also read in this chapter about Monique, who invested in her fiancé's overseas agricultural business but wasn't able to verify its status.

- Do you have any credit card debt? Student loan debt? How much? What's the interest rate for each account? How do you plan to eliminate this debt?

(No plan? Be worried.)

- How do you handle your credit card accounts? Do you pay the balance in full or only the minimum payment due each month? Do you take advantage of rewards programs? Do you pay late? Ever exceeded the credit limit? Is it time to request a limit increase? Or to switch to a card with better terms?

- Do you have any personal loans? A car loan? Motorcycle loan? Boat loan? What are the repayment terms?

- Have you co-signed a loan for anyone else? Are their payments current?

Please read Chapter 3 about the implications of co-signing.

- Have you loaned any money to friends or family members? Are you a borrower? How much? What are the repayment details?

The consequences of lending are discussed in Chapter 2, *I Loaned Money to You.*

- Do you have a mortgage? What's the interest rate? Monthly payment? How many years to payoff? Is there a home equity loan or line of credit? What are the long-term plans for that property — to keep it, do extensive renovations, rent or sell it when you get married, or live in it together? Is it a good time to refinance?

- Are any collection agencies chasing you?

Hal's story in this chapter painted the ugly picture of living with a fiancée whose creditors incessantly hassled the couple.

- Have any civil judgments been entered against you?

If you don't pay a credit card bill, a tax obligation, or a doctor's bill, the creditor may sue you. If you ignore it and do nothing, they will most likely get a default judgment. This means you lose, automatically. The creditor can take steps to enforce the judgment against you. They may be able to garnish your wages (deduct the amount straight from your paycheck) to pay the amount of your debt, plus interest and their costs. Your employer will know that you have a legal obligation that you failed to honor.

- Have you filed your tax returns every year? Paid all your taxes? Ever been audited by the IRS?

- Have you ever filed for bankruptcy? When? Why?

No one's financial background is perfect. Almost all of us have to give at least one of the "wrong" answers to these questions.

Your sweetheart may have valid reasons for prior money troubles. Issues in the past don't mean he is destined to screw everything up in the future. Maybe he was impulsive when he got his first credit cards in college, but now handles his finances responsibly.

Unemployment, a divorce, or unexpected medical expenses could have hammered your partner's savings and retirement accounts.

Please look at all the pieces of the financial puzzle. That's why you need as much objective information as possible before taking the big step forward into the Land of Together Forever.

Is there a website to find my MoolahMatch?

You know that it's critical to uncover the facts about your potential partner's finances. It's equally important to understand his or her (and your own) psychological relationship with money. A partnership works only if it's between what I call "MoolahMatches" — two people with compatible styles of handling their finances.

How do you know if you match? Refer to the Resources section for online tools that may help you understand your own tendencies as well as your partner's. For example, you can discover your "Money Personality" — are you an Amasser, an Avoider, a Hoarder, a Money Monk, or a Spender? Or try the "LifeValues Quiz" to shed some light on your attitudes, behavior, and decision-making processes.

Should your MoolahMatch be your identical financial twin, or should you look for a yin to your money yang? It's hard to generalize. It may work best if you're both frugal and work creatively to find ways to live within your means. However, it could be dreadful if you compete to out-frugal each other by measuring who uses the least amount of toilet paper. At the other end of the spectrum, two spendthrifts can quickly decimate their collective resources.

But what about the old adage of opposites attracting? If you have a spender and a saver, do they help balance each other out? Or are they setting themselves up for constant disagreement?

Call in the guys in the trench coats

Curious about someone's background, but don't want to ask them the hard questions? We all know that you can Google a person's name and find some tidbits in a fraction of a second. You'll also get hit with ads for online search companies that provide background information gleaned from public documents. Using these services, you may find past and present addresses, relatives, criminal records, pending lawsuits, or traffic tickets. Note that the data may not be comprehensive, because you have to specify the state(s) to search. You may not unearth that misdemeanor in Atlanta, the child support order in Akron, or the DUI in Albuquerque.

What about surreptitiously hiring a private investigator to check out a potential mate? I expect many of you will be opposed to this type of sleuthing.

An innovative company called InvestiDate offers workshops and webinars to teach people how to investigate their potential dating partners. They show you how to do your own due diligence (legally) to research public records, analyze social media profiles, estimate a person's income, confirm their job status and academic credentials, and interpret body language when you finally meet your date in person. You could confirm you've found your MoolahMatch!

Do you think this approach is prudent or invasive?

Prenuptial agreements: Where goes the bride?

A good predictor of whether you're destined to have arguments about money further down the marital road is how you and your fiancé handle the granddaddy of all trust issues: the prenuptial agreement.

Prenups are no longer just for rich folks. The point isn't whether you sign one. It's about the conversation you have. If your discussion is a battle of "If you trusted me, you wouldn't need me to sign" versus "If you trusted *me*, you'd have no problem signing," then consider calling off the wedding now. Things are probably not going to improve. Better to have an unpleasant fight about a prenup now than to have an even uglier divorce battle later.

I asked one person what she thought about prenuptial agreements. Patty came from a modest background, but worked in the insurance industry and did quite well financially. She was divorced but told me that if she remarried, she'd insist that her fiancé sign a prenup. "I might be a dummy but I ain't no fool," she said. "If they don't want to marry me because of a prenup, then they're not the person for me."

Just as a prenup settles in advance the financial and other consequences if a marriage goes bust, couples who live together before — or instead of — getting married might want to consider signing a cohabitation agreement. Legal protection makes sense if one person is much wealthier, if you have or plan to have children, if the partners are gay and live in a state that doesn't permit marriage or recognize their union, or if one or both partners owns a business. The laws vary by state, so have an attorney prepare a binding agreement rather than trying to do it yourselves.

If you are in an unmarried domestic relationship, it's wise to seek professional advice on key topics such as income tax, estate planning, health care and other benefits, real estate ownership, child custody, and insurance. Getting guidance on these issues is critical for couples who may lack legal protections.

Where are we going?

Whether you are considering commitment now or you sealed the deal long ago, it's important to have regular, open discussions about your financial and life goals.

What do you want to do with your money, in the near future and over the long term?

- Pay off debt?

- Take annual vacations?

- Buy a house? Supersize or downsize?

- Buy a second house?

- Invest in traditional or more speculative investments?

- Start a business?

- Save for retirement?

- Pay off a mortgage as soon as you can?

- Go back to school?

- Quit your job and embark on a new career?

- Send the kids to college? Grad school?

- Sell everything, buy a yacht, and sail around the world?

- Other?

You should also agree on practical matters such as who is responsible for paying the household bills. Even if one person is happy to be the bookkeeper and the other is relieved to be spared the monthly drudgery of this task, both of you should know where all the information is stored.

Decide how you will handle saving. Who picks the types of investments, and determines how much to invest and how much risk you can tolerate? Would it be helpful to consult a financial planner together?

Since many people handle all or most of their finances electronically, it's a good idea to keep (in a safe place) a list of all accounts, websites, passwords, and schedules of automatic payments. If something happens to the bookkeeper, his or her partner won't be left in the dark.

How do you handle the MatriMoney?

You need a plan to organize your finances. Each couple can develop a method to suit their personalities and situation. You may want to consult an attorney first, because the laws of the state where you live may dictate what happens to your assets if you get divorced, particularly in the community property states (currently Arizona, California, Idaho, Louisiana, Nevada, New Mexico, Texas, Washington, and Wisconsin). In those states, it's likely that the money you earned during the marriage becomes what I call "MatriMonial" assets, even if you kept your funds in separate accounts.

At one extreme, couples can keep all their MatriMoney separate. No joint accounts or assets, except maybe the title to the house and the mortgage. Household expenses may be split equally, or in proportion to income; for example, a partner earning 30 percent of the total household income pays 30 percent of the bills.

At the other end of the spectrum, partners can combine all their assets and debts. Everything is "ours" — not "yours" or "mine." For better or for worse, you share it all. However, even if you consolidate, it is a good idea to have one bank account and credit card in your own name. You know, just in case.

Many committed couples combine these approaches. A commingled account may be used for household and general living expenses. Each partner has total freedom to spend up to a predetermined amount — say, $250 — with no questions asked and no eyebrows raised. If you want to spend more than $250, you first discuss the potential purchase and decide together. Meanwhile, you can do whatever you want with the money in your own accounts without having to justify your transactions and get "permission."

You don't have to stick with one way of organizing your finances. Things may change over time. One couple I know started out with everything in joint accounts, but Ted became annoyed that his wife, Lulu, spent a lot of money on antiques. They decided to split up (their spending accounts, that is), and the new arrangement has worked quite well. Lulu buys and refinishes furniture and Ted is happy that he doesn't have to pay or even see her credit card bills.

No matter what approach you take, it may be helpful to have a periodic "financial summit." Review the current state of your MatriMoney and other economic affairs. Do you still agree on what your goals are and how to reach them?

What if I've already taken the plunge but didn't ask the right questions?

Suppose you're already married or intimately committed to someone, but you don't know the answers to all the important financial questions.

What do you do now? Ask. It's never too late to talk and put all the data on the table. Better to fess up now than to have your partner stumble upon the truth later.

Just because you find out that your spouse didn't reveal something doesn't mean you have to end the relationship. But you are entitled to know the truth about critical financial matters that affect your life together.

Regardless of whether you signed a prenup, it may be a good idea to sign a **post**nuptial agreement if there has been a significant financial change for you or your partner since you tied the knot — for example, if you start working after being a stay-at-home mom.

A 2012 survey by the American Academy of Matrimonial Lawyers found that most of their members who were surveyed reported an increase in demand for agreements among their already-wed clients. Of the divorce attorneys polled, 36 percent noted that it is more likely to be the wife who asks them to prepare a postnuptial agreement.

Conclusions

I know that I'm not telling you anything new when I say it all comes down to communication.

Ask the right questions, before and after you say, "I do."

CHAPTER 7

You're a Deadbeat Dad

This chapter is about the Peter Pans who engage in the most primal, intimate act, and then refuse to take financial responsibility for the human outcomes. Men aren't the only perpetrators.

Diana's story: "Where did all the child support money go?"

While we shared nachos at a casual Mexican restaurant, Diana told me about her marriage to a dud who became a deadbeat dad.

Energetic and spunky, she described herself as being "young and dumb" at nineteen when she married Bart, her high school sweetheart. After eight years of marriage they had three kids, but she left because he was sleeping around. She moved from Minneapolis to Pittsburgh, where her sister lived. Diana angrily explained to me, "I wanted to get as far away from Bart as possible."

Initially, Diana didn't bring their children with her, because she didn't have her own home. While it was extremely painful to leave her kids behind, Diana knew they needed a place to live, even if that meant staying with their alcoholic dad who often gambled away his paychecks and shacked up with a succession of girlfriends.

Bart made sure he got the child support money that Diana owed by garnishing her wages.

When she flew their three kids out to Pittsburgh to visit her, she was horrified when they told her they had no new clothes and were often left alone to fend for themselves. Her son, who was barely ten years old, often tried to make dinner for himself and his siblings. Diana checked with a neighbor in Minneapolis, who confirmed that the children were often neglected.

Diana was no deadbeat mom, so where had the thousands of dollars that she'd paid in child support gone? She was furious. Diana told me she didn't know for sure, but she strongly suspected that Bart drank it all away. Her dark eyes flashed as she crunched on the nachos.

When given the choice, the children wanted to live with Diana. Now it was Bart's turn to pay child support. At first, he lived up to his obligations, but she knew he also worked unofficially, under the table, to reduce the amount he had to pay.

It wasn't long before Bart was $20,000 behind. Diana called Child Support Services and told them where he worked. If he missed one payment from that point on, he would lose his driver's license; missing two meant he'd be looking at jail time.

Diana remarried, so it's no longer as critical that she get child support money from Bart. However, she is still annoyed. "It was the principle of the whole thing," she declared.

Maggie's story: "All my ex-husbands were deadbeat dads"

Maggie is bitter about her failed marriages to three men, all of whom shirked their child support duties.

Her life story is a complicated one, due to her ex-husbands, the children she had with each of them, and the ex-husbands' other spouses and children. I asked her to draw a family tree because I had trouble keeping track of the players in her life dramas. To further confuse things, two of her ex-husbands had the same first name. I've tried to simplify her story here as much as possible.

After Maggie's first husband Greg divorced her, he got married and divorced three more times. Including the son he had with Maggie, Greg spawned at least half a dozen children. He was always more interested in buying shiny jewelry for his new girlfriend than in paying child support.

Maggie angrily said, "He has six kids and he's responsible for none of them." At the time Maggie shared her stories with me, Greg had just married a fourth woman; they had no children together — yet.

Her second husband, Jim, left her with a pile of overdue bills and maxed-out credit cards. Jim was ordered to pay a nominal amount of child support for their son Harry. He owed an additional small amount to contribute to Harry's medical expenses, including weekly allergy shots.

However, Jim wouldn't pay. He had Harry relay this message to his ex-wife Maggie: "Tell your mother I've paid all I'm going to pay in child support." He didn't want any further personal contact with Harry.

Years later, Jim developed a relationship with their son, but Maggie spat when she told me she thought it was "a traitorous act."

Maggie managed to marry — and divorce — a third deadbeat dad. After the court ordered Bob to pay $2,000 a month in child support, he just disappeared. It took her five years to find him hanging out homeless in a Los Angeles suburb. Bob was arrested and spent four months in jail.

When he filed for divorce, Bob told Maggie and their daughter (Maggie's third child) on the phone, "This [marriage and fatherhood] isn't what I want to do anymore." He talked almost nonchalantly, like he wasn't interested in going to a movie or bowling.

Throughout all her battles with ex-husbands who refused to support their biological children, Maggie tried to get help through public agencies such as Social Services, the Veteran's Administration, Selective Service, Social Security Administration, and the police. She remained frustrated with all the government agencies and the legal system, and the lack of assistance she felt they provided for custodial parents like herself.

I couldn't help but wonder how this intelligent woman got it so wrong three times. I asked Maggie how long she'd known each husband before they got married; perhaps that data would be relevant. It didn't shed any light: She knew Greg about a year; Jim for more than two years, and Bob for seven months before they walked down the aisle. She mused, "So much for age bringing retrospection and experience bringing caution."

Elise's story: "Your dad did something bad with money"

We met Elise in Chapter 1, *You Lied to Me*, as part of the discussion about pathological liars. Her junkie husband, Jon, squandered all their money on gambling and drugs while stealing from his own father and Elise's brother. When they divorced, Jon didn't want custody of his son, but agreed to take care of Scott every other weekend and on some holidays.

It was no surprise that he didn't keep his word. Jon made excuses or said he had to work, or he took his son for only a few hours. Elise didn't mind too much because she thought Jon was a bad influence on Scott.

The court ordered Jon to pay $1,100 per month for child support. He was angry and threatened to quit his job — but was fired first. The child support payment was re-evaluated based on his income from a new temporary job and reduced to $400 per month.

Of course, Jon didn't even keep up with the lower amount. Elise tried to get the child support order enforced, but it took a long time, and then Jon lost his job again. She frequently asked him for cash; he refused.

Elise went into debt because she had to provide for her son. She often spent money from her savings account "for things that go on in life, such as school activities and prom," she explained to me. "I don't want to take things away. I want him to be happy. I want to give him as much happiness as I can, not monetarily, but socially."

When he was younger, Scott knew only that "Dad did something bad with money." At fourteen, he wanted to know more about the father who was absent during most of his childhood. Elise told Scott the truth: "He gambled everything we owned away and snorted coke up his nose." She filled in more of the grim details when he was older.

Jon didn't offer to help pay for Scott's college tuition. Despite it all, father and son had dinner together every few months and their relationship improved a bit. Jon gave his son $100 in cash now and then.

After a lifetime of drug and alcohol abuse, Jon's kidneys started to fail and he needed an organ transplant. Scott was a perfect biological match. His father pressured him to donate one of his kidneys.

Scott was torn. On the one hand, he had the opportunity to save his dad's life. But should he help the man who never did anything for his own son?

Scott struggled with this dilemma.

Ultimately, Scott refused to let Jon harvest his organs. Jon died when Scott was in his early twenties.

Elise's view was that Jon never knew *how* to be a good father. Jon's own father didn't know. She said to me, "But that's no excuse. You either become a terrific father, because yours was lousy — or you become just like him."

I know Scott personally. I am confident he will not become like Jon.

Sherri's story: "I want everyone to see who he really is"

Sherri and I got together over lunch in a cafe near Seattle. Her cousin took Kameron, Sherri's six-year-old son, to play in the park while Sherri and I chatted about Kameron's deadbeat daddy.

On a rebound from a failed relationship, Sherri met Leroy at a bar through mutual friends when she was in her early thirties. They spent a single night together, and she got pregnant. Neither one wanted to get married, or even have an ongoing relationship.

Leroy urged Sherri to get an abortion because, he told her, "It would make my life easier."

Indeed.

Sherri insisted that she would keep her baby. I didn't ask her if she had moral or religious issues about abortion, or whether she wanted to raise another child (at the time, she had a son who was twelve). It wasn't my business.

Leroy was determined to ensure that his life wasn't going to get difficult because of a baby he helped create. He continued to pressure Sherri to terminate her pregnancy. He called her all night, banged on her windows, forced his way into her house, and had other people follow her car and try to run her off the road.

Sherri's theory was that he engaged in all this aggressive behavior to terrorize her. She thought his goal was to wear her down so she'd agree to get an abortion. Or maybe all the stress would cause a miscarriage.

When their son, Kameron, was born, Leroy wasn't around; he had moved out of state. "It didn't interest him," she lamented.

Kameron has seen his father only twice in his life.

It wasn't the first time that Leroy had brought children into the world and then abandoned them. His ex-wife had three kids. He had an older son by another girlfriend. Sherri told me she thought another ex-wife or woman with a child floated around somewhere.

Oddly, Sherri had an insatiable curiosity about the mothers of Leroy's other kids. It wasn't jealousy. For whatever reason, she wanted to understand his parental life before their fateful one-night stand.

After Kameron was born, Sherri reached out to these women, and both warned her to stay away from Leroy. The ex-wife sputtered, "He's no good at all!" and told Sherri she could keep him. Sherri tried to explain that she had no use for this scoundrel either.

Sherri's other reason for tracking down Leroy's other baby mamas was to see if he paid child support. It was difficult because Leroy moved around a lot, leaving children in his wake. Despite her efforts searching the public records, she couldn't find any court orders.

I tried hard to understand why Sherri was so interested in Leroy's past. "I was just nosy," she said, a bit self-consciously. "I wanted to know what he did before. I wondered if he would help our son Kameron."

Did Sherri really think that a man who tried to destroy his child when he was *in utero* would step up and take care of him?

Sherri filed for child support. Leroy tried to convince her to drop the claim. He promised to pay her out of pocket. She knew better than to trust him.

Leroy made exactly one payment of $600 for the first month. To avoid paying more child support, he voluntarily quit his job and became unemployed. He listed bad addresses so Sherri and the authorities had difficulty tracking him down.

Typical deadbeat behavior.

Next, he claimed that the court should reduce his child support obligations for Kameron because he paid $300 per month for his eldest son's medical insurance. Even though Leroy provided no concrete evidence of this expense, the court reduced his required payment for Kameron to $400 per month. He was also ordered to pay $25 per month to catch up on the delinquent payments.

Leroy paid nothing.

One year Leroy filed his federal income tax return and was entitled to a refund. Too bad for Leroy — he didn't know that Uncle Sam could snatch it to pay outstanding child support obligations. Add $1,500 to Sherri's side of the ledger.

The saga dragged on. Once a year, the same act played out when Leroy and Sherri went to court. Leroy never provided proof of income. "He brings nothing but excuses," Sherri sneered. Once he claimed he couldn't work because he was 100 percent disabled due to back problems and sleep apnea. The judge accepted Leroy's statements without question. Every time.

Sherri was incredulous. "Ninety percent of people in this country have back problems, but they work and do what they need to do!"

I asked Sherri if she had legal representation. She didn't think the lawyers provided for her were effective. "They don't speak up for you. They just sit there and take notes," she sighed.

Once, her pro bono lawyer asked Leroy, in court, "What is your child supposed to do if you don't pay child support and he needs diapers and formula?"

Leroy's answer:

"Suffer."

Yes, that's what Leroy thought Kameron's fate was because Dad failed to support him.

His son just had to *suffer the consequences.*

Sherri was stunned.

Her lawyer restrained her from jumping over the table to attack Leroy.

The judge was unmoved. Didn't blink an eye. He ordered Leroy to pay $250 per month to catch up on his outstanding debts. Banged his worn, wooden gavel. Called for the next case. Another squabbling, unmarried couple shuffled in.

Leroy now owed almost $30,000 in back child support, not including interest.

I know what you may be thinking. Sherri was a slouch who sat around the house and lived on public assistance, right? She angled for the maximum amount of child support because she was too lazy to work.

Wrong.

Sherri wasn't on welfare. She worked full time as a clerk in a department store. "You do what you have to do," she laughed with a sad smile.

Meanwhile, Leroy was living on Easy Sleazy Street. Unofficially, he resided at his dad's expensive house with its nice manicured lawns and two new cars in the driveway. Sherri suspected that Leroy deposited any money he received into his father's account so there would be no trace of Leroy's income. This scheme allowed him to qualify for food stamps and medical benefits, but he got a pass on paying child support.

If that's not enough to make you scream, Sherri told me that when Leroy was arrested for drunk driving, he hired a good lawyer who got him out of trouble. Leroy received only probation and community service work, instead of jail time.

Evidently Leroy didn't want to spend his time picking up highway trash, so he got the volunteer hours converted to a monetary fine. Sherri estimated the amount of the fine plus the lawyer's fees totaled $10,000.

That's a lot of money that he could have spent feeding Kameron, rather than putting other people's lives at risk by driving drunk.

There's an interesting technological twist to Sherri and Leroy's story.

Sherri's cousin set up a Twitter account and a blog for her to publicize Leroy's status as a deadbeat dad.

I tried to understand her motivations in "outing" him online, using social media.

Revenge.

Sherri exclaimed, "I want to get the word out there, I want to get it known. I want his friends and everyone to see who he *really* is!"

Sherri also posted on one of the many commercial websites that exist to publicize the identities and wrongdoings of people who have allegedly shirked their child support obligations.

Many people read her posts, Sherri told me proudly. Even Leroy's father saw the online activity, but he claimed that his son was no deadbeat dad. I wasn't clear whether grandpa denied that Leroy was Kameron's father or that Leroy failed to provide for Kameron.

But it wasn't all about trying to embarrass Leroy. Sherri also wanted to help other people.

"I want to make a difference for single parents," she explained. "I'm not the only one. There are others in the same boat who can't collect child support. I even know a deadbeat mom; another woman is raising those two abandoned kids along with her own."

Sherri hoped that the people who read her blog would get the courage to keep pushing for their kids' legal rights to receive child support.

I asked Sherri what Kameron knows about his father, who has been absent virtually his whole life.

"He knows nothing. I tell him, 'God is your daddy.' I don't know what I'll say when he's older and asks questions."

Meanwhile, Sherri continued to battle on, with no success. She filed the court papers. She showed up in court. Leroy kept slipping through the system. Sherri was exhausted and frustrated.

"Staying on top of it is a full-time job," she sighed. "Leroy's living it up, and his son and me are barely making it. Where's the justice in this? Why does this happen?"

I couldn't offer any answers.

Wade's story: "My granddaughter had a deadbeat mom"

Fathers aren't the only deadbeat parents. There's no shortage of women who neglect the basic daily needs of their own kids.

Wade shared a detailed personal story with me about his son, Rick, whose life has taken a lot of unexpected parental twists over the past two decades.

When he was in his early twenties, Rick didn't know what to do with his life, so he joined the Marines. He was an alcoholic, and his drinking problem became worse while he was stationed at Camp Lejeune in North Carolina. One drunken night, he met a drug addict named Lacey at a local bar. Rick knew that she was married but slept around with other Marines and local guys. They had a short fling.

Lacey got knocked up and claimed Rick was her baby daddy. Lacey's husband Luke was a fellow Marine, and he ratted Rick out to his Commanding Officer. Because adultery can be an offense under military law, Rick was dishonorably discharged, lost all his benefits, and was ordered to have no further contact with Lacey, Luke, or their child after he or she was born.

Rick was at the lowest emotional point in his life. He wasn't interested in hanging around, so he moved to Portland where his dad, Wade, lived.

Rick heard through the Marine grapevine that Lacey gave birth to a baby girl. Her husband Luke had a paternity test, and just like when they announce on those horrible daytime TV shows ... he was NOT the father of little Melanie. Luke and Lacey promptly divorced, and Melanie stayed with her mother.

Even though she had a young daughter to raise, Lacey didn't clean up her act. She continued abusing drugs and alcohol. Lacey was strung out and sick all the time. A continual stream of boyfriends drifted in and out of her transient life. Each time a new guy moved in, Lacey told Melanie to call him "Daddy."

Any money that Lacey got her hands on — and it wasn't entirely clear what her sources of income were — paid for booze and drugs. Melanie never had enough food or proper clothes, and Lacey inflicted physical and verbal abuse on her. She gave a cruel new meaning to the "beat" in "deadbeat."

With a poor excuse like Lacey for a mother, it's no wonder that Melanie was a difficult kid. She had uncontrollable outbursts and was admitted to psychiatric hospitals periodically.

Fast-forward fifteen years. Lacey died of a heroin overdose. Her boyfriend of the month had no interest in taking care of a wild teenage girl, so he turned Melanie over to Social Services. Then he stole all of Lacey's and Melanie's meager possessions.

Melanie was alone in the world, with no family and nothing to her name.

Her deadbeat mom was dead.

For the next few years, Melanie was in and out of foster homes. No one wanted her to stay for long. She was also admitted to hospitals, and was doped up on lots of strong psychiatric medications.

When Melanie was seventeen, Rick got a summons to appear in Juvenile Court because he was potentially her biological father.

He had dreaded this moment his whole adult life.

No one is quite clear how they managed to find Rick. It had been so many years since he'd left the military and moved hundreds of miles away. By sheer coincidence, he was living about eighty miles from Melanie's latest foster home.

At the time, Rick had an eight-year-old child by another woman. He faithfully paid child support and had custody of his son every other weekend and some holidays. It was another misstep in his life, but his father Wade was glad that Rick didn't marry that woman, who Wade thought was a bit of a "loose wire."

Rick, now forty-one, went to the Juvenile Court hearing with his dad. Wade told me, "Everyone looked at Rick and me as if we were from Mars. They never expected us to show up in court."

The DNA tests showed that there was a 99.99 percent probability that Rick was Melanie's father.

I asked Wade what Rick's response was to this life-changing news.

He said Rick was "relieved." For years, Rick had lived with the possibility haunting him that he had a child. He knew he might get a hesitant knock on his front door from a girl who looked a bit like him. Maybe a lot like him.

Relieved?

Why was Rick thankful when he found out that the baby he and a junkie accidently conceived during a one-night stand turned out to be a teenager who bounced in and out of psychiatric hospitals and foster homes?

Rick and Wade saw this as a "great opportunity" to do something for this girl, who had been brutally abused by her biological mother and then passed around the government system her whole life like a hot potato.

But it didn't happen all at once. It wasn't like one of those made-for-TV movies where everyone walks out of the court together into the sunshine, smiling and holding hands as they start a happy new family.

Melanie lived in a small group home for "troubled" girls. She was improving, due to her stable environment and regular therapy. The medical team discovered that she was misdiagnosed long ago, so they discontinued the strong psychiatric medications that caused her severe side effects.

Rick and Melanie got to know each other slowly, through visits supervised by the Social Services case workers. At first, Melanie wouldn't let Rick, Wade, or any other man touch her. Gradually she grew to trust Rick and his dad, and to be comfortable with handshakes and light hugs.

Medicaid will continue to provide financial support to Melanie until she is twenty-three. Rick gives her occasional gifts and money, but he has no legal child support obligation. There's no custodial parent to pay because Melanie doesn't have — and never had — a real mother.

The current plan is that Melanie will live with Rick after she graduates from high school this year. Her ambition is to become a paralegal. She is articulate; Wade says she skillfully advocated for herself in numerous court appearances.

Rick works long hours as a hospital technician, but he got a second job to support his growing family. After Melanie moves in, he will supplement her Medicaid payments.

Wade told me he was confident that the Juvenile Court will approve this proposed arrangement. His son got his drinking problem under control and has been sober for ten solid years. Rick has proven that he is serious about his parental responsibilities. He attended numerous court appearances about Melanie's welfare.

Furthermore, the members of Rick's extended family — his young son, as well as Wade, Wade's wife, their other kids, and numerous grandchildren — have patiently taken a lot of small steps to bond with Melanie. "When it's a blood relative, you're always a parent," Wade declared.

So what did Rick — who turned out to be the exact *opposite* of a deadbeat parent — think about this whole crazy turn of events in his life?

According to Wade, Rick often says:

"It was the worst mistake I ever made, but it had the best result of all — my daughter Melanie."

Wade was bursting with pride when he talked about how his son and his granddaughter Melanie have each turned their lives around.

Now that's a deadbeat story with an *upbeat* ending.

Worst Deadbeat Dad in the U.S.

Robert Sand pleaded guilty to owing more than $1.2 million for unpaid child support, including interest and penalties. He skipped out on his obligations for three children by two ex-wives and hid out in Thailand to escape the U.S. authorities.

Since his sentencing in May 2013, Mr. Sand no longer occupies the top spot on the list of "Most Wanted Deadbeat

---

Parents" posted by the U.S. Department of Health & Human Services. The most egregious offender on the run, Joseph Stroup, owes over $559,000 as of this book's publication.

"Worst" is subjective. A deadbeat dad who owed $553,000 went to jail in 2010. His offense was particularly egregious because he'd allegedly fathered twenty-three children by fourteen women. Half a million bucks is a lot of money, but this busy man's real crime lay in affecting so many human lives. The judge branded Howard Veal as "the poster child for irresponsibility."

Enforcement

If a noncustodial parent fails to pay child support, the money can be collected in a variety of ways. The most common is automatic deductions from wages. However, this method doesn't work too well if the deadbeat parent is unemployed, underemployed, or receiving tips or other cash income that isn't reported to the IRS.

Other penalties and methods of collection include seizing sources of income such as tax refunds, workers compensation, or unemployment compensation, and suspending a driver's license or denying a passport application.

The Office of Inspector General of the U.S. Department of Health & Human Services may intervene in multi-state cases — for example, when the noncustodial parent flees the state where the child lives.

If the deadbeat has the money but refuses to pay, he or she can be fined, thrown in jail, or both. The penalties increase for repeat offenders.

Commentators have mixed views on the incarceration option. Some say it disproportionately affects destitute parents, and jailing them is counterproductive. Others say that evading child support obligations is a crime and violators should be punished.

Please consult the social services agencies in your area for the steps you need to take if you aren't receiving court-ordered child support payments.

Unfortunately, the women I spoke with whose husbands were deadbeat dads didn't have much success with enforcement and collecting the money owed to them.

Shame them into paying

Numerous websites, blogs, Facebook pages, and Twitter accounts are devoted to publicly exposing individual deadbeat parents who fail to pay child support.

Online commercial services are also available.

DeadbeatDirectory.com aspires to be "the #1 source for humiliating deadbeats of the world!" Anyone can search this website for specific individuals by name. Only members may post profiles, photos, stories, or other information they choose to share. Sign-up is free and requires only a user name, password, and email address.

Lots of heavy-duty, mumbo-jumbo legal disclaimers dominate this website. The company makes it clear they don't vouch for the accuracy of the information, which consists of "rumors, speculation, assumptions, gossip, and opinions."

The irony is that this website includes ads with links to several third-party "name removal" services. Alleged deadbeats can pay those companies to try to get their names deleted from DeadbeatDirectory.com and other online lists of deadbeats, liars, cheaters, and general evildoers. A reputation clean-up service may be useful if you think you've been unfairly badmouthed.

DeadbeatDadsFlorida.com, now defunct, wasn't a website where people freely made accusations. Instead, you paid a monthly fee but had to first provide official court documentation to show that the deadbeat's payments were delinquent. The company posted the info on its website and sent texts to the offender and his friends and family to inform them.

Do these services exist only to provide an outlet for victims to vent? Is it justified to humiliate someone online by telling only your side of the story? Doesn't this approach backfire if you make it harder for a deadbeat to get a job to pay child support?

You can report a deadbeat-on-the-run to the federal government via an official online "Report a Fugitive" form or toll-free number (refer to the Resources section). I don't know to what extent the authorities follow up, or what qualifies an offender to join their lists of "Wanted," "Arrested," or "Sentenced."

Conclusions

In Chapter 6, *I Say 'I Do' to You, Your Assets, and Your Debts*, I suggested that it's critical to do financial due diligence on your lover before you get seriously involved. You want to know, among other things, if the person (usually, but not always, a man) has obligations to pay child support. Even if his children are not your financial responsibility, their needs will affect your life.

First, if your partner has a regular monthly expense, you must include it when doing your household budget planning, just as if he had an 18-year car loan.

Second, if he fails to take care of the kids he already has, it tells you a lot about his character. He's not a keeper. Even though you're in love now and dream that you'll have children together, if your relationship tanks it's likely that he'll also duck his financial obligations for your offspring.

What if you're taking the plunge with someone who has never fathered any kids or has no history of failing to support his existing progeny? You can't predict what will happen if you later split up and you need his money to raise the children you both brought into this world.

The best protection for you is to develop and maintain marketable skills so that you can start or continue to work to support yourself and your family. Your goal is to be less dependent on financial assistance that you may never get from an ex-intimate partner.

CHAPTER 8

Where There's a Will, There's a Relative

Barbara's story: "We were one big, happy family ... and then I got nothing"

After divorce or the death of a parent, the family may grow and reshape like an amoeba, as its members re-marry, bring existing kids into the mix, and create more offspring. Their progeny grow up and may have their own kids, making the family tree ever more complex.

What happens when it all goes wrong?

One rainy afternoon in a Philadelphia suburb, Barbara told me that her close "blended" family was ripped apart in an unimaginable way.

This attractive woman was sixty-five, but looked a good ten years younger. Petite and fit, she had a soft glow about her, despite a traumatic financial event in her not-so-distant past.

It was a second marriage for both Barbara and Jeff, and each had adult children from their prior marriages. Barbara had a close relationship with Jeff's two kids, Gavin and Gail, she told me. They enjoyed celebrating holidays and events. At Christmas, weddings, and graduations, many members of this extended family showed up.

A few years after they wed, Jeff told Barbara that he needed to update his will.

This was Jeff's first critical mistake: he should have taken care of this business earlier.

Jeff's existing will was ten years old. In it, he'd left everything to Gavin and Gail (their mother had passed away). Jeff now wanted to provide for his second wife, Barbara. They hadn't signed a pre-nuptial agreement. (That's another mistake, but that's the topic for Chapter 6, *I Say 'I Do' to You, Your Assets, and Your Debts*).

Jeff wasn't satisfied with Henry, his former lawyer, so he looked for a new one to update his will and prepare Barbara's first will. However, it was one of those chores that always got pushed aside.

That's something a lot of us do, right? It's a Grown-Up task that just keeps falling further down the To-Do list. If it's even on our list at all.

Barbara avoided these discussions with Jeff, pleading, "Can't we talk about this another time? I don't want to dwell on death and dying."

Jeff and Barbara were about to travel to Peru for two weeks, and in Jeff's eyes, the new wills became a matter of urgency. The task moved up higher on his list, along with getting typhoid fever shots. He and Barbara made several appointments with a potential attorney, but they never signed any papers.

The couple returned safely from their Peruvian vacation.

Jeff was in good health, so it was a horrific shock when they found out at his annual check-up that he had pancreatic cancer. In the car from the doctor's office to the hospital, Jeff panicked about not having an up-to-date will, and he begged Barbara to find a lawyer immediately. Barbara was still stunned by the news of Jeff's terminal illness. Practical considerations were the last thing on her mind.

Jeff died five days later.

Barbara was clueless about their household expenses, debts, assets, and investments. She knew, of course, that she wasn't named in Jeff's will. His two adult children inherited the entire estate, which was worth about $150,000.

Jeff had designated Barbara as the sole beneficiary of his small pension. In addition, before they married, he named her as a 10 percent beneficiary of his IRA. Gavin and Gail were each 45 percent beneficiaries. The IRA was worth more than $500,000, and represented most of Jeff's assets.

So in total, not much money for Barbara.

Gavin and Gail were dumbfounded when they found out that Jeff had failed to update his will and IRA when he married their stepmother.

The kids reassured Barbara, her family, and their close friends that they were well aware of their father's errors and "they would take care of Barbara."

Gail, who was especially close to Barbara, told her more than once, "Just because Dad didn't do the right thing, doesn't mean we can't do something to fix it."

Barbara proposed that she, Gavin, and Gail each receive one-third of the proceeds of the $500,000 IRA. This was a generous offer; legally she could have claimed fifty percent. But Gavin and Gail rejected this proposal and made no counter-offer.

In Barbara's words, when each sibling saw that their own $225,000 payout could be reduced to $166,000, "They scurried up to the plate and took their share, like little rats."

Gavin, Gail, and their respective spouses were all successful working adults, so it wasn't as if they were destitute, she told me.

The kids suggested that Barbara prepare a budget of her income and living expenses. She was fortunate that Jeff had always kept meticulous records. Barbara admits that she was ignorant about financial matters in general; she had been willing to learn, and Jeff had wanted to teach her, but she kept putting it off. It was too late now.

Barbara received wages from her part-time job, modest income from her own investments, and Jeff's small pension. However, she couldn't maintain her current lifestyle on that income, even though she was generally frugal.

Gavin and Gail reviewed her budget and told Barbara that they weren't going to help her. At all. Her slice of the IRA pie would remain a paltry 10 percent — just $50,000 — and she would get none of the cash in Jeff's estate.

Barbara couldn't believe it. She'd thought that when Gavin and Gail asked her to prepare a budget, they intended to share the wealth — as they'd promised.

However, when her stepchildren saw they would legally inherit all of their father's assets, plus the vast majority of the IRA, they changed their tune. They wanted everything to go exactly in accordance with Jeff's unintentional plans.

Any notion of "taking care of Barbara" fell by the wayside.

"My father knew what he was doing," Gavin told Barbara, "and he was wise not to revise his will. He had no intention of doing anything for you."

Barbara retorted, "Gavin, you obviously didn't inherit your father's genes for decency. Greed is more important to you."

Gail snapped at her, "We don't know what your problem is, Barbara. You're a wealthy woman. You're certainly living above the poverty level!"

What happened to the happy extended, blended family?

Under the state laws where Jeff lived, even though his will did not provide for Barbara, she was entitled to half of Jeff's estate of $150,000, which amounted to $75,000. The bulk of his wealth was in the IRA, which was distributed strictly according to his designations, so Barbara got only $50,000 as her 10 percent share. However, her total inheritance of $125,000 was diminished by $25,000 — the amount that Barbara spent on attorney's fees to protect her legal rights.

One hundred thousand dollars may seem like a lot of money to you, and you may wonder why Barbara complained. But everything is "relative"; she got a pitiful share compared to what her relatives got. Worse, Jeff's true final wishes were not fulfilled.

Another family twist made matters even more ugly.

Jeff's will was drafted by Henry, an attorney who was an old family friend. Do you remember why Jeff was looking for a new lawyer before their trip to Peru? It was because he wasn't satisfied with Henry.

Jeff named his kids as executors of his will, so they were free to choose the probate attorney. Gavin and Gail picked Henry, despite the fact that he had limited relevant experience.

Why?

Henry's son was married to Jeff's daughter, Gail. Get the picture?

Henry couldn't be objective; his daughter-in-law Gail was a primary beneficiary of Jeff's estate. Of course he'd want Gail to get as much money as possible. Henry had no reason to do anything to benefit Barbara, whom the family had discarded like trash in the recycling bin.

Except for Barbara — who had no legal rights to pick an executor or a probate attorney —everyone chose to ignore the obvious conflict of interest.

The ultimate irony was that when Henry billed Jeff's estate for his fees as the probate attorney, his charges were in excess of what the law allowed. Barbara's lawyer caught this, so Henry backed down and reduced his bill.

For Barbara, this was conclusive evidence that Jeff's personal assessment of Henry had been correct.

Barbara got blindsided when her extended family scored money that Jeff had intended for her.

For a while, Gail tried to maintain contact with Barbara despite everything that had happened. But Barbara wasn't interested. "I felt they had betrayed me, so I had nothing to say to them," she explained to me sadly.

Is this a graphic lesson about why you should have a will, power of attorney, and other end-of-life documents that reflect your current wishes? And why you must keep your beneficiaries for IRA accounts, 401(k) accounts, and life insurance policies up to date?

You bet it is.

Barbara said that people tell her similar stories, and she understands that her situation was not unique. Barbara took some personal responsibility for what had happened:

> People said Jeff did the wrong thing, but I was equally guilty. I put it off. You have to learn by these mistakes. Life has gone on for me, although I miss him terribly. It could have been handled so much better, but there was a lack of communication as well as ignorance on my part.

Barbara missed out on hundreds of thousands of dollars. But the more heartbreaking result was the destruction of her healthy family relationships. Her blended family became pulverized. All because of poor planning and greed.

Lenore's story: "My mother-in-law stole my daughter's inheritance"

Money issues destroyed Barbara's extended family when, as the second wife, she was pitted against the biological adult children and lost.

Here's a story with the reverse result — the adult children from the first marriage (and their kids) saw their inheritance vanish, thanks to their stepmother's avarice.

Lenore was emphatic: "If you have kids, *don't remarry!*"

Is Lenore anti-marriage? No. But she has seen what happens when, even before a rich relative dies, the members of a blended family squabble about their entitlement to a future inheritance.

A real estate agent in her early fifties, Lenore has been married to Jim for nearly twenty years. Her story revolved around her wealthy father-in-law, Sam, his second wife, Sarah, and the plans the elder couple made for their golden years.

Sam's two kids, Jim and Judy, were worried when their mother died; they thought Sam wouldn't last long if he lived alone. Jim and Judy assured Sam that they didn't feel he would be disrespecting their deceased mother if he remarried. His kids just wanted their dad to be happy.

Sam had known Sarah through their church activities for many years, so it wasn't like he went prowling for a rebound partner.

"Everyone thought it would be the best thing that happened to Sam," Lenore told me, "because it would keep him alive longer." He did in fact live for another ten years after marrying Sarah.

At the time, Lenore thought that Sarah was warm, devoted to Sam, and not too concerned about money. Sarah made it clear that she married Sam for love and companionship.

Jim and his sister Judy were a bit uncomfortable with the union, because they knew Sarah had financial difficulties. She owned a house, but her late husband had left behind a slew of unpaid medical bills after he died of emphysema.

Before they wed, Sam and Sarah made a deal that was unequivocal, and all their adult kids understood the terms: "You take care of me, and I'll take care of you."

Their agreement was that Sam would make sure that Sarah was financially comfortable, both during their marriage and after Sam's death. Sam was eleven years older, so the chances were good that she would outlive him.

Sarah's part of the bargain was to take care of Sam for the rest of his life. She could hire in-home caregivers if she couldn't attend to his daily needs. Sam emphasized that he wanted to live in his own home as long as possible.

We all feel that way, don't we? There's comfort in being in our familiar environment without a lot of helpful but intrusive medical personnel hanging around. No amount of family photos displayed in your little room at the assisted living facility will fool you into thinking that you are at home.

Part of the couple's economic deal was that Sarah sold her modest house and paid Sam $300,000 of the proceeds to cover half of the remaining mortgage on his mansion. She now owned 50 percent of his house.

In addition, Sam paid $300,000 for Sarah's overdue medical debts.

However, Sam's house was worth $1.2 million, so half of it amounted to $600,000. The result was that Sarah got $600,000 in equity — *for free* — because her payment of $300,000 was a wash with the money that Sam coughed up to settle her debts.

Sam's kids knew that Sarah didn't pay half of the value of Sam's mansion, but they didn't discover until after their father's death that she'd effectively paid zero.

Jim was named as executor of his father's estate. While Sam was still living, Jim worked hard to organize the records and keep everything up to date.

He discovered that Sam had intermingled his personal funds with the money from a family trust that Sam and his first wife had set up many years earlier. The trust was for Jim and his sister Judy, plus the grandchildren (including Jim and Lenore's daughter, Laura).

Jim wasn't too worried about the mixed cash, and told his dad, "I'm not going to tell you how to manage your money." This was a generous position for Jim to take, considering that the trust funds for Jim and his family were reduced when that money was combined with Sam and Sarah's personal funds.

Sam faced the inevitable decline of his health and mental faculties. Jim and Lenore lived nearby and visited daily, but Sam needed professional in-home care and assistance. Jim had Sam's health-care power of attorney, and he worked with Sarah to arrange for more help. They converted Sam and Sarah's living room into a fully functional hospital room. Professional caregivers bustled around the house twenty-four hours a day, every day of the week.

This arrangement was difficult for Sarah, and she became quite frustrated. "I want my living room back," she said. "I don't like having other people in the house all the time. This is all very wearing on me."

Her complaints sounded reasonable, although Lenore told me that she thought Sarah played the martyr a bit too much.

Sarah wanted to move Sam to an assisted living facility, and she battled with his kids to push him out of their house. Jim wanted his dad to stay at home. Sam was calmer in familiar surroundings and it was better for his emotional health. Jim and his sister Judy were always united in their decisions about what was best for their dad.

Lenore acknowledged that this was unusual for siblings. Often when a parent is declining, the adult kids don't agree on what to do and how to handle the finances.

When Sam was eighty-seven with advanced Alzheimer's, he tripped over a kitchen chair and fell. He was admitted to the local hospital for a few weeks.

Lenore told me, "This marked the beginning of the end."

She meant the end of Sam's life, as well as the end of the good relationships Sarah had with her adult stepchildren.

The kids knew that Sarah suffered from bipolar episodes and had been hospitalized several times during her marriage to Sam. Her behavior was sometimes erratic. As Sam's dementia got worse, Sarah became more depressed. She acted hostile toward Lenore and Jim, and accused them of non-existent wrongdoings.

Sarah became increasingly stressed about her economic situation. She panicked that no money would be left for her because Sam's round-the-clock medical care was costly. But Jim did the calculations; it was no more expensive for Sam to stay at home than for him to live in a facility.

Jim and Judy pointed out to Sarah that she was well taken care of. She'd received a $100,000 cash lump sum from the recent sale of her house (in addition to the money she'd contributed to Sam's spacious home where she lived, mortgage-free), and she had a sizable income from Sam's pension, retirement, and investments. Sarah also had minimal income from her own stocks and mutual funds. The couple had no debt.

All together, she was in great financial shape. She was set for the rest of her life. Her monthly income was a cushy $10,000 — what more did she need?

Lenore explained to me that Sarah wanted to get the other 50 percent of the house. Jim and Lenore didn't understand why. Sarah could stay in the house until her death, and then her kids would inherit her half. It would have no effect on Sarah's standard of living if she owned the whole house now, whereas Sam's kids and grandchildren would lose out if she did. Sarah was trying to grab their inheritance for no logical reason.

As you see in so many of these stories, people are often motivated by sheer greed.

One weekend while Sarah was traveling, Jim and Lenore stayed in Sam's house to take care of him. Jim couldn't find the recent bank account statements. When Sarah returned, he politely asked Sarah for the documents.

Sarah went ballistic and screamed at Jim and Lenore, "You are accusing me of theft. This isn't acceptable. You're going through my private papers and yelling at me. This is verbal abuse. It's elder abuse!"

Lenore was puzzled; no one had raised their voice at Sarah. Jim was trying to be calm when he spoke with her.

During what may have been one of Sarah's manic phases, she said she needed a break. Fair enough. Caregivers have a job that is emotionally exhausting. They need to take care of themselves also.

Sarah took her entire family (twenty-eight people) on an expensive luxury cruise to the British Virgin Islands. She paid for it from her joint account with Sam, which as usual had income mixed with the trust funds.

While Sarah and her clan were living it up in the Caribbean, Jim looked for Sam and Sarah's investment account statements and credit card bills. Years of documents were missing, including the most recent ones.

Jim knew they didn't just disappear. He figured out that Sarah had removed the records before she went on the cruise, put the box in the trunk of her car, and left it at her son's house nearby.

When Jim managed to get the papers, he was astonished. Over a period of years, Sarah had systematically siphoned off a significant amount of income from the trust and shoveled it into the personal accounts.

He calculated that $500,000 was gone. Evaporated.

After the cruise, Sarah went to visit her adult daughter for a week. Then she disappeared. Completely off the grid for six weeks. One of Sarah's sons told Jim and Judy that Sarah was deeply depressed.

Sam was devastated when Sarah vanished; it made him confused and anxious.

After she returned, Sarah continued to try to remove Sam from their home. She threatened to change the locks so that Jim couldn't continue his daily visits.

Jim now didn't trust Sarah at all. Sam's condition worsened and he didn't even know that he was at home, so they all reluctantly agreed it was time to move him to an assisted living facility.

Jim and Lenore noticed that Sam's hospital and medical bills began arriving in their mailbox. They discovered that Sarah had gone to the hospital and changed the name and address of the person who was responsible for payment of Sam's account. She was trying to minimize the impact of these expenses on her future inheritance by pushing the bills to the trust. The hospital recognized the mistake and changed the bills for Sam and Sarah to pay.

During the last year of Sam's life, Sarah wanted the lawyers to change the power of attorney from Jim to her.

Sam's kids went to his regular doctor, who easily concluded that Sam was incapable of making rational legal or financial decisions. Next, Jim and Judy called in their attorneys. They won that battle and the power of attorney wasn't changed.

However, the relationships between Sarah and Sam's kids went south after everyone lawyered up.

According to Lenore, "None of us tried to get our hands on any money that Sarah was entitled to. We fought only to keep the half of the house that belonged to our family. Sam's kids had only ever wanted to fulfill their dad's desire to live at home for as long as possible."

Jim and his sister Judy saw that the family trust with their future inheritance was evaporating, as Sarah continued to drain the trust fund account.

Lenore told me that the kids weren't concerned if they didn't inherit much, because Sam had allowed the financial intermingling. At the same time, Jim and Judy knew Sam and their mother wouldn't have intended to disinherit them and the grandchildren, but they didn't know how to stop the train.

Jim and Lenore agreed that Laura's grandparents would want her to get her share of the trust funds, so they fought to preserve their daughter's stake.

Lenore described herself to me as "feisty," but this wasn't her fight. She loved her father-in-law and had always had a great relationship with him. But while she was sure that Sam wouldn't want a protracted battle, she also felt he wouldn't want young Laura and the other grandchildren to lose out.

During a few moments of lucidity six months before his death, Sam turned to Jim and said, "I haven't seen Sarah for a while." It was true that Sarah hadn't visited Sam at the assisted living facility for a few days. Jim and Lenore told a little white lie for Sam's benefit and reassured him that Sarah faithfully visited.

Sam continued, "You know, I think that I made a mistake. What I thought she was going to do was not what happened."

Jim and Lenore were speechless. They had never discussed Sam and Sarah's arrangement with Sam, and they had no idea what Sarah had ever said to her husband.

Yet somehow Sam knew that Sarah hadn't lived up to her end of their life bargain.

Sam passed away peacefully three years ago, in the presence of Sarah and his kids.

After paying all the legal fees, medical bills, and taxes, Jim and Judy each inherited about $350,000. The half a million dollars that Sarah had diverted was long gone. Laura got a small amount from the trust, about $25,000, for her future education.

Recently Sarah wrote Jim a note that said something like, "I'm so sorry about all the fights and troubles we've had. I know I said some inappropriate things to you. It was all because of my depression. Can't we patch things up?"

Jim wasn't impressed, so he just ignored Sarah. Lenore told me that her husband will be bitter forever because Sarah embezzled $500,000 from the trust, hid the bank statements, and tried to get their half of the family mansion.

I asked Lenore what she thought about Sarah's efforts to apologize and make amends with Jim.

"If she feels that sorry, she can give the money back," Lenore responded tartly.

Sarah had always had a close relationship with Jim and Lenore's daughter Laura, but things became awkward after Sam's death. Laura was torn, wanting contact with Sarah but sensing the tensions between her parents and her step-grandmother and not understanding why.

When she was a bit older, Jim explained to Laura that he was furious with Sarah because she'd schemed to steal the money that Laura and her cousins were entitled to inherit.

Sarah and Laura continued to visit. Sarah occasionally gave her step-granddaughter some cash, perhaps $100 for her birthday or Christmas, and Laura was happy with those gifts.

Lenore's husband Jim grumbled that Sarah should give her more because she'd depleted Laura's trust fund. He sputtered that Sarah's gifts were like a payoff. Blood money. Yet Jim and Lenore tried to stay out of Laura's way and let her make her own decisions about the rocky evolution of her relationship with Sarah.

As far as Lenore was concerned, the moral of her blended family's story was:

> If kids are involved, *don't remarry*. Live together. Love each other all your life. Share your money if you want to. Make sure the second partners will be taken care of after death. But don't remarry, because it affects everything. It creates inheritance challenges. All the adult kids are thrown into disarray. If Sarah and Sam had simply lived together, it would have preserved all the family relationships and everyone's resources.

I asked Lenore about her own family situation — her dad had remarried after her mom died. While there wasn't nearly as much money in play as in Jim's family, her dad (who is a lawyer and CPA) made sure that all the legal documents, including a prenuptial agreement, were in place and that funds were properly segregated.

Whenever her dad updated his will and trust documents, he gave copies to Lenore, her brother, and their stepmother. Everything will be clear for Lenore's brother when he becomes trustee and executor of their dad's estate.

With this transparency, everyone knows who owns what now and what the future arrangements will be. Her dad even sold or gave away his stamp and coin collections, so there will be fewer assets for the family to distribute after he is gone.

As for herself, Lenore recognized that because Jim is older, the odds are that he will predecease her. Having another intimate relationship was hard for her to imagine, but she remained resolute that she won't marry again. She didn't want her daughter Laura to witness more family fights.

In the end, the big pot of money was diminished because of all this unnecessary drama. A lot of cash went to the lawyers, instead of benefitting anyone on either side of Sam's or Sarah's family.

Ezra's story: "My sister has delusions of entitlement"

Ezra was working out of state when his father suddenly passed away. He wasn't sure (although he doubted it) whether his father had a will. After Ezra returned home, his younger sister Leah appointed herself as executrix of their dad's estate. But she didn't file any of the necessary papers with the probate court. Ezra also thought she removed all bank statements and other financial records from the house and didn't let anyone see them.

"When I asked her about it, Leah said that all the funds were exhausted when she paid $20,000 for our dad's funeral costs," Ezra told me. He was dubious, and believed that Leah had siphoned off the cash for herself.

Ezra couldn't afford to consult a lawyer, but did his own legal research and concluded that the state laws would allow him to petition the probate court for an accounting of the funds. He felt that whatever money was left should go to his aging mother — not to his sister or even to him.

He was adamant that things be handled properly. Ezra told me, "I want to see the money end up in the right place — to the bill collectors and the funeral home. Not to my sister. Leah has always had delusions of entitlement."

At the time of our meeting, Ezra was still trying to learn the ins and outs of probate court to see what his legal options were to make things right.

The richest woman with a slapdash will

Huguette Clark (pronounced "ooo-GET") was the richest woman you have probably never heard of. Fiercely protective of her privacy, she was a copper-mining heiress and philanthropist who died in 2011 without any children, grandchildren, or siblings.

In the last years of her life before her death at age 104, she caught the public's attention. It was revealed that she'd given lavish gifts of cash, houses, cars, jewelry, paintings, a Stradivarius violin, and other priceless assets to her caregivers and advisors, including her private nurses, doctor, lawyer, and accountant.

Her story was the subject of the *New York Times* bestseller *Empty Mansions: The Mysterious Life of Huguette Clark and the Spending of a Great American Fortune,* written by Bill Dedman and Paul Clark Newell, Jr. (Huguette's cousin). Meticulously researched, with numerous photographs of Madame Clark, her family, properties, and other possessions, this definitive biography has been optioned for a feature film.

Wealth, greed, politics, scandal, priceless art, family feuds — you've got it all in one century of one person's life.

It's a true story of a reclusive woman with unimaginable wealth who chose not to enjoy what her money could buy. How inconceivable it is to us that she owned but never occupied several mansions on both coasts that were painstakingly maintained and filled with original paintings.

Instead, she chose to live in a simple hospital room for the last two decades of her life, despite being in quite good health for a centenarian.

Imagine the spectacular battles between the people who were supposed to inherit, and those who felt they were entitled. The stakes in the Clark estate were much higher due to the vast sums of cash and valuable assets involved.

Most people are quick to criticize that she gave her day nurse more than $30 million. However, the nurse, Hadassah Peri, cared for Huguette twelve hours a day, seven days a week, fifty-two weeks a year — for twenty years. That's not the typical schedule for a caregiver who is not a blood relative.

The relevance for us ordinary folk is that this woman of breathtaking wealth ignored — for years — her lawyers' advice to update her will.

After their persistent nagging, she signed a will, and then a different version six weeks later. The latter will was unequivocally clear that she left nothing to family. She was well aware that the vultures were circling her hospital bed not long before her death; relatives who had never met her in person tried to cozy up for a visit. She gave strict orders to the hospital staff barring all family members.

Beneficiaries included her doctor, attorneys, accountant, assistants and property caretakers, and the Corcoran Gallery of Art in Washington, DC. Huguette also established an arts foundation to receive her Santa Barbara mansion and paintings.

The situation was complicated, at best. People who were excluded from the will alleged that Huguette was manipulated or coerced by her professional advisors, who had received unusually high salaries for years.

Nineteen relatives challenged Huguette's will. Over $300 million was up for grabs. They claimed their distant relative had been fleeced and defrauded by advisors and nurses. Surely she wasn't mentally competent when she signed the will that cut out her entire biological family, they maintained. However, none of the relatives had seen her in decades, if ever. They had no basis to judge her mental condition at the relevant times.

A settlement was reached in September 2013, just before an expensive, lengthy legal process would have begun.

The big winners? The family and the arts foundation. The losers? The lawyer, the accountant, and the nurse. While Nurse Peri didn't inherit the $30 million she was promised, it wasn't a huge loss. She and her family had received the equivalent amount over her lifetime of caring for Huguette, although she did have to repay some of the excessive cash gifts.

The story may never end. Huguette's former night nurse sued, claiming Huguette had promised to provide for her also.

Major questions will persist, perhaps forever. What were the elderly Madame Clark's true intentions? Was she coerced and financially exploited during her lifetime? Or just an eccentric and generous benefactor who was genuinely appreciative of her service providers?

We may face similar questions about the people in our lives, even though the stakes are lower. How do we know where to draw the line?

Her child was older than she was

One unusual and complex true story involves an heiress, her lesbian partner, an adult adoption, a predictably big squabble when it was time to divvy up the multi-million-dollar trust funds, and myriad lawsuits.

Olive F. Watson was the granddaughter of the founder of the giant technology company I.B.M., and her father was the company's CEO. In the early 1990s, when Ms. Watson was forty-three, she adopted her long-time lesbian partner, Patricia Ann Spado. The heiress adopted Ms. Spado, who was actually one year her elder, to ensure her partner would be a beneficiary of certain Watson family trusts. At the time, same-sex partner benefits were virtually non-existent.

From the start, it's hard to wrap your head around this story where the middle-aged adopted daughter was chronologically *older* than her same-sex lover/parent.

This drama played out in Maine, where the Watson clan summered. At the time, Maine was one of the few states that allowed an adult to adopt his or her same-sex partner; New York, where the couple lived, did not. In fact, New York didn't permit adoption as a way for unmarried couples to legalize their relationship, whether they were homosexual *or* heterosexual.

Unfortunately, all didn't go well with the Watson/Spado relationship. They broke up less than twelve months after the adoption. Apparently Olive didn't try to undo their union; it may have been legally irrevocable.

More than a decade later, it was time to divvy up the Watson family fortune, including among eighteen grandchildren who were beneficiaries of various trusts. Olive had no children.

Wait — but she did, right? Patricia Spado was her legal offspring and, as the nineteenth Watson grandchild, entitled to a share of the riches.

Not so fast, said the Watsons, who tried to get the adoption annulled. They argued that the law wasn't intended for gay adoptions, the couple didn't live in Maine, and Olive's father never knew about the odd arrangement. Ms. Spado's entitlement to her share — worth between $5 million and $15 million — was the subject of lawsuits that circulated around various courts for many years.

I included the Watson/Spado story here even though it's so specific that it's unlikely to be relevant to your personal situation.

Instead, it serves as fair warning to LGBT (Lesbian, Gay, Bisexual, and Transgender) couples that there's a minefield to maneuver through if you want to achieve the same rights and protections as traditional male/female spouses. At the date of publication, same-sex marriage is legal in fewer than half the states, although the landscape continues to change. The laws about gays or lesbians adopting their partners vary as well; some states flat out prohibit it, and some require that there be a minimum age difference between parent and child, regardless of gender.

Where permitted, a marriage or a domestic partnership is more likely — but not guaranteed — to withstand challenges to inheritance rights than one of these awkward adoption arrangements.

Same-sex couples should get tailored legal advice on estate planning and other critical family issues.

Family feuds: From dysfunctional to worse

Death can bring out the worst in the survivors. There's nothing quite like the loss of a relative — particularly a parent — to bring a family together in grief, and then tear it apart when everyone reads the will. Family members who got along reasonably well for decades can get downright ugly when it's time to divvy up a departed relative's money and property. Old sibling rivalries emerge. As Ezra said, referring to his sister, "Everyone thinks they're more worthy."

Siblings who are incensed at what they think is unfair may rationalize their positions:

"Why did Linda get as much as I did? I earn a lot less than she does, so I need more money."

"Of course I should get a larger share. My wife and I took care of Mom for years. Where were you?"

"Dad paid for Bob's grad school tuition while I worked to support myself, so Bob's portion should be smaller."

The problem of perceived unfairness in inheritances is more complex and often worse in second or later marriages.

Remember, where there's a will, there's always a relative who shows up.

Amanda's story: Who was the beneficiary of the life insurance policy?

Amanda and I talked over dinner at a popular local Italian restaurant. She was in her mid-thirties, looked considerably younger, and closely resembled Nicole Kidman. You'd never guess that this poised, self-confident, and successful stockbroker had ever had any sort of financial problems.

When they were only twenty years old and nearly broke, Amanda and Randy got married in Georgia. Randy was in the Army, and one of his benefits was a life insurance policy. Randy's mother was the original beneficiary, but he told Amanda that he'd updated the policy so she'd receive the benefits. On several occasions, he reassured her, "Don't worry, if I die, you'll get $100,000."

Randy left the military, but they kept the insurance policy. Uncle Sam was no longer footing the bill for that benefit, so the couple paid the premiums out of their joint account. Amanda also worked, but her married life wasn't happy. Randy was cheating on her, and he was an abusive bully.

Eventually, she kicked him out and moved from Georgia to Tallahassee, where her sister lived.

A few weeks later, Randy was killed in a motorcycle accident.

Who was the beneficiary of the $100,000 life insurance policy? Randy's mother.

Amanda was shocked to discover that she'd be getting nothing. Absolutely nothing. She was still Randy's wife; they had been married for almost five years and weren't divorced, or even legally separated.

The Army wouldn't tell her anything. His family didn't help her. They were in denial that Amanda had left their son because he was unfaithful. Randy's current girlfriend attended the funeral and was treated like she was the grieving widow, instead of Amanda.

Was Amanda *ever* the beneficiary of Randy's insurance policy? Or did he change it back to his mother after Amanda left him? She'll never know.

Amanda flipped her blond hair and told me how Randy's family later tried to reach out to her. They sent "We love you" cards and emails. She didn't respond.

What was she supposed to say?

Amanda was angry about their past behavior. She wasn't ready to confront her former in-laws with her unanswered questions: "Why did you treat me like that? Why didn't you give me anything? Why wasn't I entitled to some help to start over?"

Their sudden interest confused her. Why did they care about her now? What had changed?

Life insurance: You're worth more when you're dead

If you have a life insurance policy, you choose the beneficiary — the person or people who will receive the big pile of money when you die.

The payout isn't intended to be a lottery prize. The money should go to someone (usually your spouse or kids) who, before you died, depended on your income to pay for their living expenses.

Reevaluate your choice of beneficiary if you have a life-changing event, such as when you (re)marry, divorce, have children, or if your beneficiary dies before you (this is why you name a "contingent," or back-up beneficiary, in case you forget to change it after your primary beneficiary dies).

Some state laws address how a divorce affects the provisions of your will. It's possible that your ex-spouse may be automatically removed as the beneficiary, even if you didn't tell the insurance company.

It could be a nasty surprise if you assumed you were the beneficiary of a life insurance policy and then you didn't get the cash. I doubt Amanda ever got legal advice about her rights as Randy's lawful wife when he was killed in the crash.

Financial life after death can be complicated.

To pull the plug, or not?

A friend of mine had a freak accident and fell into a deep coma for days. The team of doctors couldn't agree on his chances — would he die? How long should they wait to see if he woke up? If he regained consciousness, what would his physical and mental condition be? Could he improve? Or would his quality of life be severely compromised? Should his family "pull the plug" and let him fade away in peace?

My friend Gregory hadn't signed any documents to address this situation. Not even a will. I'm sure he didn't intend to leave a mess for his family that would affect all of them forever.

I'm happy to tell you that Gregory did wake up. At first, he had severe short-term memory loss and physical complications. With a combination of hard work, patience, the love and support of friends and family, his religious faith, and a lot of luck, he's recovered more than even the most optimistic doctors predicted. He'll never be the 100 percent pre-accident Gregory we knew. But it's a heck of a lot better than the alternative.

On the topic of incapacity, you may remember the story of Terri Schiavo. Hers was an extreme example of the problems that can arise if you don't leave proper instructions. She was suspended in a vegetative state for fifteen years. Because she hadn't signed a power of attorney or advance directive, a bitter and extraordinary public court battle was waged over whether her feeding tube should be removed. Her husband was pitted against her parents about who had the right to decide. Her feeding tube was removed, reinserted, and finally removed in accordance with a complicated series of court orders. No one wants a judge to determine whether you live or die.

What does any of this have to do with economic exploitation?

It's a nauseating situation to consider, but you could be a fatal victim of financial abuse if someone stands to benefit from your death and they've got the power to disconnect you. Perhaps you would have wanted to hang onto this life a bit longer.

Please — if you will, don't die without a will

Many people don't want to confront the inevitable fact. Face it, you're going to pass away, kick the bucket, expire, shuffle off this mortal coil, and die ... someday. Definitely. If you do nothing to prepare for the legal niceties, here's what happens: the state decides who gets your money and possessions. You'll cause a lot of headaches and unexpected work and expense for whoever is left behind. Is that really what you want to do?

Even if you think you don't own a lot of valuable stuff, or you believe (perhaps incorrectly) that your spouse and kids will inherit, you are doing everyone a great disservice by not expressing your last wishes in a proper legal document.

Without a will, you die "intestate." This doesn't mean you've got an awful gastrointestinal disease, but rather that the government will distribute your money and appoint a guardian for your minor children.

More than half of adult Americans don't have a will

A Harris Interactive® for Martindale-Hubbell® research study in 2007 found that 55 percent of all adult Americans didn't have a will. The numbers were lower among African American and Hispanic adults.

Meanwhile, in 2012, a survey by RocketLawyer.com found that 41 percent of Baby Boomers — adults aged fifty-five to sixty-four — hadn't signed a will.

You can prepare a will and other end-of-life documents, such as powers of attorney and advance directives, without a lawyer. Loads of information and documents are available online, for free or for a small fee.

Personally, I shudder at the thought of cutting corners on what may be the most important pieces of paper you will ever sign.

But if you are dead-set on doing it yourself, please make absolutely sure you get at least one detail right: the will must be valid in the state where you live (your "domicile"). This is critical, because each state has different laws. Something as simple as not having your signature properly witnessed and notarized could cause your entire will to be declared invalid — and all because you insisted on taking the cheap route.

When you hire an attorney, choose one who specializes in estate law. Your brother's divorce lawyer isn't the best choice to prepare your will or trust.

While we all want to work with an experienced professional, my view is you *shouldn't* hire the senior partner in the law firm. Why? I want an attorney who has a better chance of outliving me. I prefer that the person who prepared my will and understood my intentions still be around when it all matters.

Prepare yourself thoroughly before you set foot in the attorney's office to get your estate documents drawn up. First, sit down, take a deep breath, and ask yourself these questions:

- What do I own? Not just cash and tangible things. Include your digital assets, such as photos, email, computer files, and online accounts such as social networks.

- Who do I want to get these items?

- Do I want to leave any money to charities? My alma mater?

- Who will be the guardian for my minor children? Do I want any restraints, such as stating that the kids can't get the money until they are twenty-five years old, or that the money can only be spent on higher education?

- Who do I want to make health-care decisions for me if I can't?

- Who will take care of my pets? Fido can't "inherit."

- Do I want to donate any of my organs or tissues for transplantation? Or donate my whole body for medical research and education?

- Do I want an autopsy to be performed?

- What kind of funeral arrangements do I want? Burial? Cremation? What sort of memorial service?

- Do I want an obituary to be published in local newspapers? In my alumni magazine?

- What about setting up an online memorial for friends and family to contribute photos and stories about my life?

Well, that was fun, wasn't it?

The single most important question is this: Who will be the executor of your will or trustee of your trust? That person (called a "personal representative" in some states) gets the tedious and thankless job of organizing the paperwork, corresponding with the courts, paying your debts, distributing your assets, and dealing with your heirs (or the people who think they *should* be your heirs).

It's best to name only one person as your executor. Parents sometimes name two or more of their children as joint executors because they don't want to favor one over the other and are convinced that the kids will agree on what to do. My view is that this is asking for disaster. Remember, money makes family members act funny (and not in the ha-ha sense).

A close friend and neighbor with a terminal illness recently asked me to be co-executor of her will with her cousin. I told Serena I would do anything in the world for her — but not that. I cannot agree to share this critical task with her blood relative who lives thousands of miles away.

She assured me that her cousin (whom I've never met) is nice, reasonable, intelligent, and wealthy.

I don't care. He doesn't know me. He may question my motives or how I know "what Serena would have wanted." If he's too busy or lazy to do the paperwork, I have a legal responsibility to get it done. I'm willing to be her sole executor, her contingent executor (in the event that her cousin is unable to fulfill his obligations), or someone with no legal status who can help because I live in the same county as Serena. But I'm not going to be a co-executor with him.

I don't want something to write another book about.

Famous people who died without a will

Here's a list of well-known people (many of whom were also well-off) who died intestate: Abraham Lincoln, Bob Marley, Pablo Picasso, Amy Winehouse, Barry White, Sonny Bono, and Stieg Larsson (author of *The Girl With the Dragon Tattoo* series).

Can you imagine the protracted battles that ensued among their relatives, partners, business associates, creditors, and friends?

Don't end up like them, even if you don't have a fortune.

Keep your will and trust documents up to date. Getting divorced? The states differ on what the effect is vis-à-vis your ex-spouse. Getting married? Don't forget to change the beneficiaries for your IRA, 401(k) plan, and life insurance. Remember Barbara's true story about what can happen if a will and other documents do not reflect your current wishes.

You can also learn from Barbara's experience that if your spouse handles the household financial matters, it makes good sense to understand all the pertinent details while he or she is still around to discuss them with you.

For starters, make a list of all bank and investment accounts, insurance policies (auto, home or renters, life, health, disability, long-term care, and umbrella), mortgages, and loans (student, auto, personal, business).

Because many people receive and pay their bills online, you need to specify what arrangements you have set up. Do the utility bills get deducted automatically (and from which account?) or do you pay them manually?

Where have you stashed away the family's important papers, such as birth certificates, marriage and divorce certificates, Social Security cards, military discharge papers, car title, house deed, and original wills?

You may wonder about the connection between death and financial abuse.

It all comes down to whom you pick to carry out your wishes — can you trust them, despite their own financial interests, if any? Are you confident they'll make sure that the people you want to inherit your stuff will get it?

Recently I updated my will and other end-of-life documents.

It made me stop and think about a lot of things. My money and material possessions. My complex relationships with friends and family. My priorities. My health. My spiritual beliefs. What sort of legacy I want to leave. Whether or how I want to live if the unimaginable happens. Who I predict will outlive me. What people will think about me and my choices (although I guess I shouldn't worry too much).

There's plenty of information available online about end-of-life and disability topics.

My attorney recommended the Consumer's Tool Kit for Health Care Advance Planning, compiled by the American Bar Association's Commission on Law and Aging.

The documents in this kit are *not* legally binding. Instead, you use them to let your family, close friends, and doctors know now what your personal medical preferences are.

There's so much more to consider than just a generic coma-type situation. The kit has you ask yourself a series of questions. For example:

- Do you want to be an organ donor? (My answer: Yes)

- If you have Alzheimer's disease, do you want to be fed by a stomach tube? (My answer: No)

- Would you be willing to endure the unpleasant side effects of chemotherapy if it could prolong your life? (My answer: Uncertain)

You fill out the questionnaires and store them with your will and other important papers (be sure to tell your family where you put them).

The kit also includes a "proxy quiz," for your family members to ask themselves how they think *you* would answer the questions. The goal is to see if they know your preferences. If your family gets it wrong, now is the time to educate them — before they've got thorny decisions to make.

Bottom line: having your written instructions in hand may prevent unpleasant arguments later among your relatives about your wishes.

An advance directive tells relatives and health-care providers what you want if you can't tell them. You can specify in a living will what types of medical treatments you would agree to.

Sign a health-care power of attorney and name someone you trust to decide about your medical care.

Conventional advice says you should sign a general durable power of attorney to grant the person you choose a wide variety of rights, such as the ability to write checks on your accounts and to sell investments. However, be aware that some banks and other institutions won't honor a one-size-fits-all document, even if a lawyer prepared it for you. They don't want to spend time figuring out what it says and whether it's legally binding. They may worry about their liability if they get it wrong and let some rogue clean out your account.

Instead, many banks have their own form of power of attorney. The better practice is for you to sign one at every individual bank, financial institution, or brokerage where you have an account. The person you name will have a much easier time taking care of your financial affairs if they're holding the papers that the bank accepts.

Another option is "payable on death" accounts. You specify who gets the bank account or CD when you die, so there is no need for a power of attorney. An advantage to this option is that the account bypasses the probate process. The beneficiary has no rights to the account while you're alive, and you're free to change the beneficiary, spend the money, or close the account.

The law requires you to name your current spouse as the beneficiary of 401(k) and pension plans. You can bypass your spouse and name someone else only if your spouse agrees in writing. "Honey, please sign this waiver and I promise, you won't get a penny." Not likely.

Conclusions

Life and death situations are unpredictable. The issues are rarely black and white. Even if you have all your paperwork in order, you can't cover every possible scenario.

There is no way to predict how people will behave when their loved one dies or has a life-threatening emergency. They will be faced with excruciating decisions to make at a highly stressful time.

Make it a lot easier for them. Spell out what you want.

Most of us ignore or procrastinate checking these cold and clinical tasks off our to-do lists.

Pick up dry cleaning — check.

Get the car inspected — done.

Sign your will and other morbid documents ... maybe next week. We just don't want to be confronted with the possibility of our mental and physical decline and inevitable death.

Please put your preferences in writing and discuss these gruesome details in advance, because you won't be able to speak for yourself later.

Make sure all the important people in your life do the same, in case you're left behind when *they* depart.

CHAPTER 9

I've Got Grandma's Checkbook

None of this could ever happen to me

OK, so you think none of this stuff about financial disasters applies to you? You're in a long-term, stable relationship. You and your partner are open and honest about the household economics. You don't lend money and you're not willing to co-sign for anyone. You even have your will and estate documents in order. (I'm impressed!)

Stay tuned, because you are indeed at risk.

Imagine that your spouse dies before you. It must be terrible to outlive your beloved partner and be the last one standing. Or suppose you don't have a significant other.

As you age — alone — you start to get a bit foggy upstairs. You think slower, move slower. You forget more than just where you left your glasses or the car keys. Eventually you become dependent on a caregiver, perhaps a relative or a hired professional. That person helps you handle your money and pay your bills.

How will you know if he or she is acting in your best interests or robbing you blind?

The short, sad answer is that you may not know.

No one I spoke with was an elderly victim of financial exploitation. Instead, concerned family members told me what was happening to their relatives and how they felt powerless to stop it — even through the social services agencies and the legal system.

Financial abuse of senior citizens is in a lonely category in this book. When you're the victim, you often don't see it and can't stop it. But you can learn how to act to protect yourself and to recognize the warning signs if someone else appears to be a victim.

Steven's story: "You're supposed to make sure all their needs are met"

A divorced, unemployed technician in his mid-fifties, Steven told me about a whopping combination of inheritance and elder issues in his family. He uncovered the disturbing details when he moved back home to Houston after he lost his job in Dallas.

Steven's mother suffers from a combination of dementia and mental illness. She is ninety-three and lives alone, but her two children visit every day. Steven's older sister Andrea is their mother's primary caretaker and claims she has a durable power of attorney, but Steven hasn't ever seen it. If the power of attorney is valid, Andrea can control their mother's finances and make health-care decisions for her.

Andrea told him that she instituted a "do not resuscitate" order. If their mother has a heart attack or a stroke, no heroic medical efforts will be made to save her. Steven was horrified and angry that Andrea didn't consult him about this life-or-death decision. Did Andrea even discuss it with their mother?

Dad died a few years ago, and Steven believes Andrea helped herself to whatever funds were left in their parents' joint checking account. Their mother's Social Security benefits checks arrived like clockwork on the second day of each month. His sister always ensured she was there to deposit them into their mother's account, and then she wrote checks payable to herself and forged Mom's signature.

Steven told me he knew this was going on because his mother was clearly incapable of visiting the bank or filling out and signing a check.

Andrea has even easier access to their mother's Social Security income now that it's electronically deposited. No more waiting for the paper check to arrive, no trip to the bank.

Direct deposit is convenient, but for all the wrong reasons in this case.

Steven is 100 percent correct that if you have power of attorney to handle someone's personal affairs, "You're not supposed to give yourself a salary — you're supposed to do it out of the goodness of your heart."

In addition to stealing money, Andrea neglects to take basic care of their mother's house.

When Steven first returned home, he cleaned up the overgrown yard, planted a garden, and vacuumed up several years' worth of dust in the house.

If Andrea needs light bulbs, she removes them from her mother's lamps. It makes no sense. Andrea isn't struggling financially. She inherited $250,000 when her husband died and then cleaned out their dead father's accounts. Andrea receives Social Security disability benefits and freely spends her mother's limited funds.

Yet she's so stingy she won't buy new light bulbs for herself or her mother.

Steven has limited income, but he's the one who buys batteries for his mother's smoke detectors and other small necessities.

He's disgusted and described his sister as "a sponge who's cheap and would rather fill up her daughter's gas tank before taking care of the needs of her own mother."

Mom is supposed to take medication to control her high blood pressure. Steven checks the bottle of pills when he visits, but it never looks like the quantity has changed. Andrea says she has a new prescription; he thinks she doesn't want to spend the money to fill it even though the pills are inexpensive.

At one point, Steven said that he thought that Andrea might be withholding the medication in a cruel attempt to hasten their mother's death. Later in our conversation, he backed off that theory and said he thinks Andrea is "merely" a selfish miser.

Steven was calm when he recounted his family stories to me, but I could tell that he was concerned and frustrated. I asked if he had confronted his sister. He hasn't; he's worried that Andrea may retaliate by interfering with his ability to land a new job. He can't afford to stay unemployed, but at the same time Steven can't bear how Andrea treats their mother and uses her alleged power of attorney "as a license to steal."

However, Steven wasn't just standing by as his mother's personal life slid downhill.

He studied the state laws to determine what his rights and options are if his sister abuses the power of attorney and neglects their mother's basic care. He will ask the court to eject his sister and put him in charge of his mother's legal and financial affairs.

Steven understands what it means to be a caretaker for an elderly person. "I want to put everything the way it *should* be. You're supposed to make sure all their needs are met and not put them at risk."

He wants to keep the lights on.

Faith's story: "All I want is for him to be protected"

When a victim of elder financial abuse has memory issues, it can be difficult or even impossible to determine whether he or she was exploited. The details of this story are a bit murky, which unfortunately is common in scenarios involving senior citizens.

On a sunny day in Chicago, Faith told me a complicated story about her aged father, who is nearly ninety-five and lives alone in a small English town.

Her father is intelligent and well-spoken, but has mild dementia and certain undiagnosed mental illnesses. He is a troubled, complex man who has distanced himself from his only child, Faith. At best, their relationship is precarious.

About five years ago, during a period of relative lucidity, Faith's father told her that his cousin Max was helping him with some paperwork. Faith never knew she had a second cousin named Max. Her father had always been extremely secretive about his personal life, but still it was odd that no one had ever mentioned this member of her family. The genealogy was complex, and she spent hours untangling the family tree before she determined that Max was probably the son of Faith's grandfather's sister.

Gently trying to get more information, Faith asked her father about the papers that Max was helping him with. He told Faith that he'd just found out he inherited, from a distant relative, a small cottage in the English countryside. This was yet another piece of mysterious family history. The property had belonged to someone on her father's maternal side. It's not clear how Max even knew about it, because he belonged to another tangled branch of the family tree.

Max was pleasant enough the first time Faith spoke with him on the phone. It turned out they were about the same age, and he had lived in Chicago years ago, but now lived near London. Faith pressed him about the cottage and asked why and how he'd become involved. Max said only that Faith's father had asked him to help locate the property and get the documents straightened out. To date, it had cost Max about $15,000 in legal expenses, but he said Faith's father refused to pay him. Max told her that her father threw his gnarled hands in the air and said, "Max, why don't you just take the old property and be done with it."

After some thought, Faith found she didn't buy his story. It wasn't believable that her father wouldn't reimburse Max for the expenses; it wasn't his way at all.

Later Faith got upset and sputtered at Max, "I don't know you, I don't know who you are, but I am shocked that you didn't contact me about a family matter that is so important." Max replied glibly that her father was clear that he didn't want to discuss it with his daughter.

Faith explained to me that on one hand, Max's story was plausible because her father was always such a closed book. But after having told his daughter part of the story of this property, why did he refuse to talk about it now? She was baffled and had a bad feeling about the whole matter. However, she reflected that it was possible her father had indeed decided to give Max the property — but that she could never prove anything either way.

Faith's father lives in his own small house and has a caregiver who looks after him during the day. The caregiver was instructed to contact Faith in case her father's health worsened or if anything "unusual" happened.

Faith became alarmed when the caregiver called to report that Max and a lawyer were at the house and her father was signing documents. The caregiver did not know exactly what the papers were about, but she sensed that something was amiss.

Angry about this latest intrusion into her father's life, Faith called Max and demanded an explanation. What had her father signed? Where were her father's copies of these documents? Why was a lawyer there? Did her father even understand what he was doing? Max explained that the routine paperwork was necessary for her father's health insurance.

The caregiver found the lawyer's business card and passed the details to Faith, who called and peppered him with questions. But the lawyer cited attorney-client privilege and said he couldn't discuss his client's (Max's) business with her.

Faith was furious. "My father is nearly ninety-five years old and is clearly not of sound mind, and you made him sign important papers?" She threatened to have him disbarred. The lawyer backed down and admitted that her father had signed a general durable power of attorney in favor of Max. The lawyer said he would ask Max to return the power of attorney to her father.

But Max refused. He told the lawyer he wasn't afraid of Faith.

The caregiver found copies of other papers and forwarded them to Faith. She believes that Max used the power of attorney to get the property transferred to himself. Cousin Max now owns the cottage that her father was supposed to inherit.

Faith was disgusted and told me, "He was very greedy. He bullied an old man to get the title documents for a small property that is not even worth much."

The sad story didn't end there. For many years, Faith was a signatory on all her father's bank accounts. His expenses were modest and relatively consistent. She rarely checked the statements. However, her experience with Max led her to examine them more closely. She noticed numerous larger withdrawals, which was odd because her father never handled much cash.

The amount of the withdrawals beyond his normal expenditures added up to almost $60,000 over a two-year period.

Faith couldn't prove it, but she thought that Max had influenced her father to come up with the cash to reimburse his "legal costs" for the property. You know, the cottage that Max now owned.

The timing of those withdrawals coincided roughly with the period when he was hot on the scene "helping" her father. She knew that Max had a low-paying job and three kids to support and send to college.

When we spoke, Faith hadn't given up. She'd hired a lawyer to see if they could get the property back, due to Max's fraud and his attorney's unscrupulous and incompetent actions. Dealing with all of these problems was expensive, time-consuming, and difficult for her to accomplish from another country, thousands of miles away.

Meanwhile, her father's mental condition was continuing to deteriorate. He grew more fearful and paranoid. Faith didn't talk with him about this whole dreadful situation. It would upset him and he might think that Faith had ulterior motives. "I just want him to be protected from being taken advantage of," she said to me.

Faith kicked herself for being duped initially by Max's smooth talk. She pointed out that con men get you by gaining your *con*fidence.

To this day, she's not even sure whether Max is part of her biological family.

She hoped that others would read her story and be skeptical of "long-lost relatives" who show up with their eyes on a big prize.

Chin's story: "I hope my dad dies in his sleep"

Chin, a wealthy real estate broker in his mid-fifties, told me that his elderly father gave him power of attorney for all his health and financial affairs. Chin dutifully retitled all his father's assets, bank accounts, credit cards, car title, and insurance policies into both their names. This would enable Chin to better manage his dad's business now and in the future if his dad was unable to take care of things.

But his younger sisters Mia and Ling thought Chin had tricked their father into this arrangement so Chin could take advantage of poor Dad. The daughters passionately expressed their concerns to their father and convinced him to invalidate Chin's power of attorney.

How did the sisters get him to change his mind?

Fear.

Mia and Ling said that Chin would stick Dad in a nursing home for the rest of his life.

Of course, Dad panicked. Who wants to be left alone in an institution to die?

Chin told me he was annoyed that he had to undo all the pains-taking paperwork that he did to take care of their father's affairs.

His sisters believe they saved Dad, because now Chin couldn't interfere in his personal business or steal from him while he's still alive.

No one could help Dad now.

Chin admitted to me that he hoped his father would die in his sleep. Otherwise, if he gets sick or is incapacitated, none of his children will be able to make any important health-care or financial decisions on Dad's behalf.

I know Chin personally, and I believe his motives were genuine. At his father's request, he helped him with his personal business.

But these types of situations with aging parents and their adult children do raise a lot of thorny questions.

Who would act in Dad's best interests?

Would Chin have helped himself to his father's cash, since he had instant access to the accounts?

Were Mia and Ling jealous that their father didn't choose one of his daughters?

Was their father mentally competent to decide for himself whom he could trust?

Problems of the rich and famous (or rich but not so famous)

The stories that people shared with me about elder financial abuse involved everyday, ordinary folks. These events could happen to any of us — we could be the elderly victim or the powerless family member.

Wealthy people are not immune, and may in fact be more at risk.

The well-known Manhattan philanthropist Brooke Astor became the most famous victim of elder abuse to date. The socialite's only son, Anthony Marshall, was accused — by *his* own son — of stealing, withholding money for his mother's medications, and allowing her to live in absolute squalor. He was cleared of the abuse charges but had to give back approximately $12 million in cash, jewelry, and artworks. Marshall was convicted in 2009 (two years after his mother's death at 105) of pilfering her $185 million fortune by means of fraud, conspiracy, and grand larceny while she suffered from Alzheimer's disease.

The Astor case is distressing, and not just because of the sordid details of theft and alleged physical neglect. You can't help but think, if these atrocities could happen to a prominent member of our society, what hope do the rest of us ordinary citizens have that something similar won't happen to us?

While Brooke Astor was once the doyenne of New York society, Huguette Clark was a virtually unknown heiress when she died in 2011 at age 104 without any direct descendants. Chapter 8, *Where There's a Will, There's a Relative*, includes a summary of the battles for inheritance of her $300 million estate.

The Huguette Clark case made for a salacious story and a *New York Times* bestseller that will be made into a Hollywood movie.

Our own lives are not so dramatic, of course, although there is a common thread.

When you expose older people and their money to friends and relatives, it can be unclear how to distinguish between a coerced victim and a generous giver.

Elder abuse: The crime of the twenty-first century?

Americans are aging; the Baby Boomers are downshifting. All generations are feeling the effects of national (and international) economic hard times. Combine that with an "entitlement" mentality and you have the perfect storm for unscrupulous people to take advantage of vulnerable seniors and snatch their money, assets, or property.

Typical examples include relatives who pressure an aging man to change his will, or a "friend" with no prior close connection to a widow who suddenly gains power of attorney and legal control over her personal affairs.

I was unable to interview any elderly victims of financial abuse for obvious reasons — they often don't realize what is happening to them and if they do, they're terrified to speak out.

The people who contacted me were family members who, like Steven, witnessed what was happening to a relative and felt unable to do anything.

Paul Greenwood, Deputy District Attorney for San Diego County, speaks tirelessly nationwide about the mistreatment of our senior citizens. He declares that elder abuse is "the crime of the twenty-first century." Mr. Greenwood has been involved in the prosecution of more than two hundred felony cases of physical and financial elder abuse and obtained six first-degree murder convictions (yes, you read correctly: *murder*.).

His experience alone is compelling evidence that countless elders of both genders and across all socio-economic, racial, religious, and ethic groups are victims. Types of abuse include physical, sexual, psychological, and economic. Quite often a complex combination of cruel behavior is involved. Perpetrators can include family members, friends, caregivers, attorneys, financial advisors, legal guardians, and workers in assisted living facilities, nursing homes, and hospitals.

It is sickening how many opportunities there are to take advantage of defenseless senior citizens.

Like other abuse victims, the elderly may decide not to report what happened to them because they are ashamed or fear retaliation. But the added complication is that older people are getting — well, *older*. The result is a gradual decrease in their physical abilities and mental agility. Seniors may be faced with additional disadvantages when they become socially isolated. Often they are forced to rely on predators who are in an opportune position to injure or exploit them through trickery, fraud, coercion, or intimidation.

Statistics? No reliable figures exist. The studies and research I found did not even have a consistent definition of "senior citizen." Do your Golden Years begin at 60? Or 65? Additionally, various states have different ways of defining abuse and collecting data. Financial abuse is sometimes lumped in with other types of exploitation. Plus, how can we know the true extent of the problem if it is, as everyone agrees, largely unreported?

Fortunately, awareness of elder abuse is growing and further research is being conducted, including research specifically about financial issues. Organizations such as the National Center on Elder Abuse, the National Committee for the Prevention of Elder Abuse, the Center of Excellence on Elder Abuse and Neglect, and the National Network to End Domestic Violence provide a wealth of information and resources for the public, such as how to spot the warning signs and where to report all types of suspected abuse.

How can you recognize elder financial abuse?

It is difficult, maybe even impossible, to know if your friends or family members are exploiting you, as an elderly person, for their own profit.

It's critical to know if the older people you care about are potential victims.

The experts list numerous warning signs or symptoms that may indicate abuse. There are two broad and overlapping categories: significant fluctuations in assets and changes in financial behavior, and an increased involvement by other people in the senior's life.

Sudden shifts in funds may be cause for suspicion — for example, if money is disappearing from accounts either on a regular basis or in lump sums, contrary to the person's regular banking habits. Another possible indicator of abuse is atypical credit card charges. Something may be afoot if the elder has sufficient income or funds, but his or her standard of living has deteriorated — imagine Steven's mother sitting alone in a dark house.

It's also cause for concern if the senior citizen signs a will, power of attorney, contracts, or other legal documents that may have critical financial ramifications. Steven doubted that his mother ever executed a will, but he knew that "if she did, she would not have understood the meaning of it."

The other warning sign is when new friends suddenly appear on the scene and take a concentrated personal interest in the senior citizen.

Considerate neighbors may help out by doing grocery shopping, cutting the lawn, or driving to medical appointments, without it being cause for concern. But watch out for the schemers who worm their way in so they can accompany the elderly person to the bank or the ATM and then scoop up the cash withdrawals. Or those scoundrels who threaten or convince the seniors on some phony pretext to hand over money, jewelry, or other valuable property, to give them power of attorney, or to include them in a new will. Look also at the financial and social circumstances of the potential abuser. It's common for abusers to be jobless or junkies (or both).

Experienced elder abuse prosecutor Paul Greenwood draws a consistent profile for crooks who prey on the elderly. If we made a movie, picture a Seth Rogen–type character: the typical unemployed, lazy son in his forties or early fifties who lives at home with his mother. She enables him by doing all the cooking and cleaning; he has no motivation to move out. He's either a confirmed bachelor who never left home, a divorced guy who claims he can't afford to pay both alimony and rent for his own apartment, or he just got out of jail.

He keeps asking Mom for money, and eventually she confronts him. Sonny becomes physically violent and hits her. She's too ashamed to call the police or tell anyone because — well, he's her dear, darling son. He continues to abuse her, she continues to protect him, and one night he beats her up so badly that she lands in the emergency room. That's when the police get involved.

What can you do to protect others?

On a regular basis, visit a family member or a nursing home resident to check in and maintain personal contact. You can involve community professionals, for example asking religious leaders to inform their congregations about the problems of elder abuse.

If you believe that an elderly person has difficulty managing their finances, consider hiring a trustworthy professional money manager. Not an investment advisor, but someone who can help the senior budget and pay bills. Perhaps a local community organization offers trained volunteers.

Don't hesitate to contact Adult Protective Services and other social services agencies in your state if you believe an elder is being exploited. The APS caseworkers are usually the first responders when abuse, neglect, or exploitation of vulnerable adults is reported.

The National Center on Elder Abuse provides a comprehensive list of helplines, hotlines, and prevention resources, organized by state. Resources for help include the Eldercare Locator (a national agency provided as a public service by the U.S. Administration on Aging), and, for those residing in a facility, the National Long-Term Care Ombudsman.

If you suspect elder abuse — trust your instincts. Don't delay; it could mean the loss of money, health, or life. Don't hesitate to dial 911 if you believe a person of any age is in immediate physical danger.

What can you do to protect yourself from strangers?

This book focuses on what unscrupulous friends and relatives do. However, because of the magnitude of elder financial abuse, I've also addressed situations where strangers prey on senior victims.

Paul Greenwood, the California white knight prosecutor who specializes in elder abuse crime, recorded a YouTube video for mmLearn.org with ten tips, summarized below.

1. Don't hire an in-home caregiver from a newspaper or online advertisement. Use only a licensed, bonded agency. Don't rely on personal references; insist that the caregiver agency give you copies of their background checks. Greenwood explained that many of his cases involved convicted felons who found a lucrative gig as a "caregiver" and did a lot more taking than giving.

2. Jewelry is the easiest thing for someone to steal when they are in your home, so keep your precious items locked up. Make an inventory and include photographs.

3. Shred any paper that has personal information.

4. Keep your mailbox secure or get a post office box. Thieves will take credit card statements because they often include blank balance-transfer checks. If you reorder checks, pick them up at the bank instead of having them sent to you. An obvious box of checks in your mailbox is an unmistakable invitation for a thief to steal money from your account.

5. Check your credit reports several times a year at *annualcreditreport.com*.

6. Make sure that all phones have Caller ID. Be cautious if you see "Private," "Unknown," or "Out of Area," because

it may be a crook calling. Hang up if you are unsure. To discourage annoying telemarketers, blow a whistle into the phone when they start talking. Unfortunately, that won't stop the "robocallers."

7. Foreign lotteries are always a scam. Beware of bogus checks payable to you that arrive in the mail, even if they look legitimate. Correspondence with many spelling mistakes and grammatical errors is a warning sign.

8. Arrange for your bank to send a copy of your monthly bank statements to a trusted family member or financial advisor. It's helpful to have another pair of eyes review the transactions.

9. Don't assume that a contractor or handyman is licensed, bonded, and qualified to do repairs at your home. Check with the Better Business Bureau. Does your state or city require a license? Make sure the person you hire holds that license — and that it's up to date. Get three estimates for any work before you hire. You and the contractor must sign a written contract. Don't pay a high up-front deposit. Take photographs of the work in progress.

10. Always have a second line of defense at your door. Install a screen door, peephole, or chain so you can block someone from entering. Never let anyone in, even if it's a young, innocent-looking woman with a cute baby. If you allow a stranger to enter your home, he or she could ask you to get

something from another part of the house, which leaves the stranger free to steal your wallet or other valuables.

A critical preventative step is to plan your financial future now. Get your what-happens-if-I-can't-take-care-of-myself affairs in order. Read Chapter 8, *Where There's a Will, There's a Relative*, about the issues of incapacity and inheritance and how you must be proactive to spell out your preferences.

Experts agree that elder abuse occurs to senior citizens who become vulnerable because of their social isolation. So avoid dependency on a single person in your life. Develop and maintain a network of your close friends and relatives. Stay connected.

Conclusions

I have only scratched the surface about the issue of financial exploitation and abuse of our senior citizens. It's a problem that will only get worse as we all get older. There is so much more we need to learn in order to prevent, recognize, and stop it.

10 Tips to Prevent Friends and Family from Ruining Your Finances

The 10 tips

If you jumped to this part of the book thinking you'd find all the magic answers, you'll be disappointed.

Sorry.

There are no foolproof ways to prevent or deal with all types of financial exploitation by your partners, friends, acquaintances, or relatives.

In addition, I've raised difficult questions for you that I haven't answered.

But don't let the gold diggers, deadbeat dads, and Credit Cads win!

Sexually Transmitted Debt, Empty Accountitis, and other conditions that result from financial abuse are not incurable. You may not be "infected" or affected forever. You can recover. You can survive. You can achieve financial wellness and thrive.

Prevention is always better than a cure, so be proactive.

Based on my own experiences, the true stories I heard from my volunteers, and what I have learned along the way about personal finance, I suggest the following ten general tips. None of them are novel. It's all common-sense advice that you have heard elsewhere.

1. Read contracts and other legal documents before you sign them.

2. Don't sign anything you don't understand.

3. Don't agree to financial transactions if you are being pressured.

4. Don't marry or commit to another person until you've asked all the key questions about money and are comfortable with the answers.

5. Share all relevant financial information with your partner.

6. Don't lie to your partner about important things.

7. Be alert for the signs that your partner is deceitful.

8. Sign your will and other estate documents and tell people what you want, because one day you won't be capable of making decisions or expressing your wishes.

9. Stay connected with your friends and family members. Don't become isolated or dependent on a single person.

10. Help our senior citizens live their final years with dignity and the respect they deserve.

You can find lots of detailed and useful information about all the individual topics in this book at reputable personal finance websites run by knowledgeable bloggers and writers.

Final conclusions

The stories in this book aren't pretty. The endings are not tidy and happy.

The people I interviewed represent only a tiny sample of the millions who have experienced financial misfortunes caused (at least in part) by a spouse, partner, friend, co-worker, or family member.

What's the silver lining, if any?

A few of the people who shared their tales with me waxed philosophical and felt that even bad experiences could have positive outcomes.

As Monique said after she broke off her engagement to Felipe, "This will make me stronger as I go on with my life. I should count my blessings, not the negative things that have happened to me."

Amira, who loaned all her money to a manipulative boyfriend, said, "I didn't die. The world didn't end." The upside was that she felt that she could now depend on herself, rather than relying on a man to take care of her.

Barbara, the widow whose husband neglected to update his will to provide for her, reflected and told me, "You have to learn by these mistakes. Life has gone on for me."

Even the victim of one ex-husband who was a deadbeat dad and another ex-husband who was physically violent was optimistic.

"Every day, it gets better." LaShanda said. "I've come a long way and I'm only going to get better."

My husband conned me out of my life savings and covered up critical details about his assets for a decade. I started over and saved diligently for years to rebuild my finances.

The best part is that I no longer see myself as a victim.

I feel privileged to write a book that I hope will reassure people they aren't alone if they got their assets kicked. I also hope this book can help prevent readers from making bad money moves.

As all the compelling stories in this book graphically illustrate, you must carefully consider with whom you are getting in bed when you mix your close personal connections with your financial obligations.

Love, trust, and money raise a complex blend of issues in your family, intimate, and other social relationships.

Good luck. I wish you many years of financial and personal happiness!

Postscript

The stories never end.

Whenever I post on my blog, a reader writes me, or I talk with someone about this topic, I hear more tales of financial abuse and exploitation.

So this book doesn't end here. There's going to be a sequel, *Gold Diggers and Deadbeat Dads 2: More True Stories of Friends, Family, and Financial Ruin.*

Stay tuned: Maybe someday you'll see *Gold Diggers and Deadbeat Dads: The Movie* in a theater near you.

As always, if you'd like to share your story with me, the same rules apply. I'll change all names, places, professions, and other identifying details in my best efforts to protect the innocent (and the guilty). Contact me at *valerie@valerierind.com.* I'd love to talk with you.

Acknowledgements

To my family and close friends: Your unwavering support for more than half a century is priceless to me.

To Helaine Becker: You believed in me as a writer long before I believed in myself.

To Sheba Meland: Your editorial input was invaluable.

To Leslie Morgan Steiner: You gave me the courage to tell the world.

To all the amazing people who shared their personal stories with me: You are not alone. Thank you for your honesty, bravery, and desire to help others.

Resources

The resources below are listed in the approximate order in which they are mentioned in the text.

While the author and publisher have made every effort to ensure these links are accurate, up to date, and relevant, the author and publisher cannot take responsibility for pages maintained by external providers.

Chapter 1: You Lied to Me

Linn, Allison. "Sometimes We Cheat on Our Partners About Money, Survey Shows." *Today*. TODAY Money, 24 Apr. 2012. Web. 21 Sept. 2014. <*http://lifeinc.today.com/_news/2012/04/24/11291884-sometimes-we-cheat-on-our-partners-about-money-survey-shows?lite*>.

Perron, Rebecca. "AARP Bulletin Survey on Financial Honesty." *AARP*. AARP Research, Oct. 2012. Web. 21 Sept. 2014. <*http://www.aarp.org/money/investing/info-10-2012/financial-honesty-couples-money.html*>.

"Financial Infidelity Poses Challenge for Couples." *NEFE*. National Endowment for Financial Education, 14 Feb. 2014. Web. 21 Sept. 2014. <*http://www.nefe.org/press-room/news/financial-infidelity-poses-challenge-for-couples.aspx*>.

Feldman, Robert, *The Liar in Your Life: The Way to Truthful Relationships* (New York: Twelve, 2009).

Forward, Susan, Ph.D., *When Your Lover is a Liar: Healing the Wounds of Deception and Betrayal* (New York: HarperCollins Publishers, Inc., 2001).

Fehlberg, Belinda, *Sexually Transmitted Debt: Surety Experience and English Law* (Oxford: Oxford University Press, 1997).

Chapter 2: I Loaned Money to You

Prosper. *Prosper.com*. Prosper Funding LLC.

Lending Club. *LendingClub.com*. LendingClub Corporation.

U.S. Small Business Administration. *SBA.gov*.

ZimpleMoney. *ZimpleMoney.com*. Zimple, Inc.

Chapter 3: I Co-signed for You and Got Sexually Transmitted Debt

Lawton, Jenny, "What is Sexually Transmitted Debt?" Summary of Proceedings, *Women and Credit: A Forum on Sexually Transmitted Debt*, Victoria, Australia, 6 Mar. 1991. n.p. n.d. Auspiced by the Victorian Consumer Affairs Committee. Co-ordinated by the Ministry of Consumer Affairs. Print. Cited *How to Get Out of Sexually Transmitted Debt*, a guide published by WISER (Women Investigating Social and Economic Reform), 1990.

Fehlberg, Belinda, *Sexually Transmitted Debt: Surety Experience and English Law* (Oxford: Oxford University Press, 1997). Cited Women and Credit Task Group, *How to Get Out of Sexually Transmitted Debt* (Melbourne: Consumer Credit Legal Service, 1990).

U.S. Federal Trade Commission. "Your Equal Credit Opportunity Rights." *FTC.* Web. 21 Sept. 2014. <*http://www.ftc.gov/bcp/ edu/pubs/consumer/credit/cre06.shtm*>.

Chapter 4: You're a Gold Digger

Seeking Arrangement. *SeekingArrangement.com.*

Sugar Daddy For Me. *SugarDaddyForMe.com.*

"Are You a Gold Diggin' Woman?" *Blogthings.* Blogthings. Web. 21 Sept. 2014. <*http://www.blogthings.com/areyouagolddigginwomanquiz*>.

Chapter 5: You Also Physically Abused Me

Littwin, Angela K., "Coerced Debt: The Role of Consumer Credit in Domestic Violence," *California Law Review* 100 (June 1, 2012).

Chapter 6: I Say 'I Do' to You, Your Assets, and Your Debts

Annual Credit Report. *AnnualCreditReport.com.* Central Source, LLC.

myFICO. *Myfico.com.* Fair Isaac Corporation.

National Endowment for Financial Education. *NEFE.org.*

National Foundation for Credit Counseling. *NFCC.org.*

Association of Independent Consumer Credit Counseling Agencies. *AICCA.org.*

Mellan, Olivia. "Money Personality Quiz." *Moneyharmony.* Money Harmony. Mar. 2012. Web. 21 Sept. 2014. *<http://www.money harmony.com/MHQuiz.html>.*

"LifeValues Quiz." *Smartaboutmoney.* National Endowment for Financial Education. Web. 21 Sept. 2014. *<http://www.smartabout money.org/lifevaluesquiz>.*

"InvestiDate: How to Investigate Your Date." *Investidateyourdate.* InvestiDate. Web. 21 Sept. 2014. *<http://www.investidateyour date.com>.*

"Postnuptial Agreements on the Rise Says Survey of Nation's Top Divorce Lawyers." *AAML.* American Academy of Matrimonial Lawyers, 10 Sept. 2012. Web. 21 Sept. 2014. *<http://aaml.org/about-the-academy/press/press-releases/pre-post-nuptial-agreements/postnuptial-agreements-rise-says->.*

Chapter 7: You're a Deadbeat Dad

The United States Attorneys Office, Eastern District of New York. "Most Wanted 'Deadbeat Parent' Sentenced to 31 Months' Imprisonment for Fleeing to Evade Over $1 Million in Child Support Obligations." *Justice.* U.S. Department of Justice, 21 May 2013. Web. 21 Sept. 2014. *<http://www.justice.gov/usao/nye/pr/2013/2013may21c.html>.*

Office of Inspector General. U.S. Department of Health & Human Services. "Child Support Enforcement." *OIG.* Web. 21 Sept. 2014. <*https://oig.hhs.gov/fraud/child-support-enforcement*>.

Little, Lyneka, "Ultra Deadbeat Dad Gets 23 Months in Jail." *ABCNews.go.* ABC News Internet Ventures, 29 Sept. 2010. Web. 21 Sept. 2014. <*http://abcnews.go.com/Business/michigan-father-23-kids-jailed-paying-child-support/story?id=11747999*>.

DeadbeatDirectory. *DeadbeatDirectory.com.*

Office of Inspector General, U.S. Department of Health & Human Services. "Report a Fugitive." *Forms.* Web. 21 Sept. 2014. <*https://forms.oig.hhs.gov/hotlineforms/fugitive-form.aspx*>.

Chapter 8: Where There's a Will, There's a Relative

Dedman, Bill, and Newell, Jr., Paul Clark, *Empty Mansions: The Mysterious Life of Huguette Clark and the Spending of a Great American Fortune* (New York: Ballantine Books, 2013).

Jacobs, Deborah L. "Adult Adoption a High-Stakes Means to an Inheritance." *NYTimes.* The New York Times, 20 May 2009. Web. 21 Sept. 2014. <*http://www.nytimes.com/2009/05/21/your-money/estate-planning/21ADOPT.html?_r=0*>.

Adoption of Patricia S. 2009 ME 76. Maine Supreme Judicial Court. 23 July 2009. Print.

"Majority of American Adults Remain Without Wills." *Lawyers.com.* Lawyers.com, 3 Apr. 2007. Web. 21 Sept. 2014. <*http://press-room.lawyers.com/Majority-of-American-Adults-Remain-Without-Wills.html*>.

"In a New Era of Estate Planning Rocket Lawyer™ Survey Shows That Only Half of Adults Have a Will." *Rocket Lawyer.* Rocket Lawyer, 28 Mar. 2012. Web. 21 Sept. 2014. <*http://www.rocketlawyer .com/news/article-Make-a-Will-Month-2012.aspx*>.

"Consumer's Toolkit for Health Care Advance Planning." *AmericanBar.* American Bar Association, Commission on Law and Aging. Web. 21 Sept. 2014. <*http://www.americanbar.org/ groups/law_aging/resources/health_care_decision_making/consumer_ s_toolkit_for_health_care_advance_planning.html*>.

Gordon, Meryl, *Mrs. Astor Regrets: The Hidden Betrayals of a Family Beyond Reproach* (Boston: Houghton Mifflin Harcourt, 2008).

Chapter 9: I've Got Grandma's Checkbook

Annual Credit Report. *AnnualCreditReport.com.* Central Source, LLC.

National Center on Elder Abuse. *ncea.aoa.gov.* The Administration on Aging, U.S. Department of Health & Human Services.

National Committee for the Prevention of Elder Abuse. *PreventElderAbuse.org.*

Center of Excellence on Elder Abuse & Neglect. *CenterOnElder Abuse.org.* University of California, Irvine, School of Medicine.

National Network to End Domestic Violence. *nnedv.org.*

Eldercare Locator. *Eldercare.gov.* The Administration on Aging, U.S. Department of Health & Human Services.

National Long-Term Care Ombudsman Resource Center. *theconsumervoice.org.* National Consumer Voice for Quality Long-Term Care.